THE NEW THING

Cutting-Edge Ideas for 21st Century Ministry from Progressive Leaders in the Wesleyan Heritage

THE NEW THING

Cutting-Edge Ideas for 21st Century Ministry from Progressive Leaders in the Wesleyan Heritage

Alan E. Nelson, Ed.D.

Contributing Editor

The Southwest Center for Leadership
Scottsdale, Arizona

This book is dedicated to friends of this project,
Mike and Sheila Ingram, who are examples of a growing number
of lay leaders burdened for the future of our churches and desiring
to see our local congregations progress into the 21st century.

Chess is a metaphor for 21st century leadership because of its complexity. The strategy is to align a team with members of varying capacities and abilities in order to accomplish a singular objective in an ever-changing playing field.

Southwest Center for Leadership: Developing 21st Century, Value-driven, Servant Leaders

Contents

The 29th Day

What is the future of your church? In his book, *Death of the Church*, Mike Regele says this:

> What about the literally thousands of churches across America in which no progressive strategies are attempted? Let's be frank. In reality, many of them will not see the dawn of the twenty-first century. Many more will pass away by the end of the first decade. We have looked at the demographics. There is no future for most. Let's stop the denial!
>
> No one wants to close a church. There is something fundamentally wrong about it. We feel as if we have failed. Making matters worse, those remaining in churches that need to close are inevitably dear old saints. The prospect of "taking their church away from them" doesn't make any of us feel particularly heroic! So we look for new churches to stay and tell ourselves a little tale that goes like this: "When people get older, they come back to church. We just need to wait for the young people to come and care for all these little churches."
>
> But the changes transforming our world reflect more than the young who have temporarily wandered away to "sow their oats." They are not coming back, certainly not in numbers large enough to pail about thousands of empty shells. The data simply do not support it, and the transformational changes that are occurring support that data. The place and role of the church in America has changed, and we will not go back! We just haven't accepted our death yet. [1]

Regele's words are pretty strong and seemingly melancholy, but as an experienced demographer, he knows what many of us are in denial of—our churches are not "cutting it."

Many of us in evangelicalism sense that things are not as they were, but we're not quite sure what it is that needs to change or how to change it. We think there is time to wait it out. Perhaps the good ol' days will return. We confuse Pollyana-like blindness with faith. Our situation can be compared to water lilies in a pond. Water lilies can reproduce quickly and overtake a body of water. On day one, a single lily pad floats. The next day, there are two. On day three, four; and day four, eight. On day twenty-nine, half the pond is full of lily pads. The naive observer may note that the pond is only half full of lilies, not realizing that tomorrow, day thirty, the pond will be totally consumed by the plant.

It is day twenty-nine in the holiness movement. Although many of us have prided ourselves on our theology, believing that our conservative, biblical teachings would keep us from the downward spirals of our mainline friends, we were wrong. Our fault is that a majority of us have fallen out of touch with our culture and have lost a missionary mindedness. Our doctrine will not save us if we lose our connection with a lost and dying world. Many look at our denominations and say, "Sure, things could be better, but half the pond is still lily free. Don't worry. Don't be melodramatic and suggest we change too significantly. Let's just fine-tune what has worked in the past. Let's just beat the old program drums a little louder. Maybe we can exorcise these demons which are keeping us from growing." And so, we pretend that day thirty will never come, at least not for a long while.

The "C" Word

Now as never before, major shifts in ministry, evangelism, and church life are taking place. Recent years have revealed a new move of God to reach people. Like all people throughout history, they are in need of His love. But unlike previous generations, these people are post-Christian, post-modern, and cannot be connected with previous methodologies. We can curse the changes or we can make assertive adjustments. Our decision will determine whether or not we survive in the 21st century, let alone thrive.

But what's gone wrong? Sometimes my wife and I are sitting in adjoining rooms, reading or working on individual projects. We interrupt each other with a comment, question or story. Occasionally, one of us leaves the room and the other starts talking, oblivious to the fact that there is no one next door listening. Our earnest words float into an empty room.

A majority of our churches are talking to neighbors who have left the room. We assume that our communities are hearing us as they have in the past, but we begin wondering why people are not beating down our doors. What's wrong with them? Don't they know they need our message? They must certainly be shunning God because they're not responding. We take on a separatist mentality, suggesting that we as Christians should not go too close to a society which is going further and further from the ideals of Christ.

> We too often use the theological and biblical compromise as a red herring for confronting the real issue. What is the real issue? We don't want to confront the degree to which we have enculturated the Gospel and our traditions. The real issue is this: It is not the core of our message nor our identity that is at stake in the widening gap. It is our cultural comfort zone. [2]

The problem isn't the unchurched or society in general. It's not the responsibility of the lost to seek the church. It is the church's responsibility to do what it takes to reach them. The problem is us. We've not taken the time to notice that no one is there to hear our messages of the past. We must move to where they are if we are to communicate. Moving toward them does not mean leaving our truths. We take them with us, but we must move closer to people in hopes that they can hear our message and hopefully believe in our God and love Him.

What is even more scary than Regele's indictment of evangelical measures at reaching people, is that his study includes holiness circles. When looking at what newcomers (who are not just transferring from other traditions) feel about our churches, few had interest in holiness churches. In fact, of seventeen church group categories considered to be most and least preferred by unchurched newcomers, the holiness category was least preferred. We ranked far behind New Age, Buddhist, Unitarian, Jehovah's Witness, Non-denominational, and Pentecostal, and not far behind Mormon, Baptist, Judaism, Lutheran and Catholics. Although the studies date to 1993, I see little change in our attitude or behaviors since then, which would imply we may be even worse off than the studies reflect.

Years ago, trains dominated the transportation business. But then came planes, superhighways, and more reliable cars and trucks. Train companies thought that if they just marketed trains better, the competition would not hinder them. Unfortunately, the train industry is nearing extinction. Officials thought they were in the train business, when in reality they were in the transportation business. Likewise, many churches think they are in the church business, the keeper of traditions, steeples and organ music sales. Many have forgotten that we are in the soul-growth business, which involves spiritual communication and helping people connect with God. If we don't step back, see the big picture, and think about why we do what we do, we will go the way of the trains and so many other outdated organizations.

To tap The New Thing and align ourselves with God for 21st century ministry will require us to change (the "C" word). The idea of change should not threaten us. New things are a part of our theology. People say, "But God never changes. He is the same today, yesterday and tomorrow." Right, and it is the character of God to create, to constantly do new things for new times and new people. God didn't stop creating after the first six days. He's never stopped doing new things.

> *"He put a new song in my mouth, a hymn of praise to our God. Many will see and fear and put their trust in the LORD" (Psalm 40:3).*
>
> *"See, the former things have taken place, and new things I declare; before they spring into being I announce them to you. Sing to the LORD a new song, his praise from the ends of the earth, you who go down to the sea, and all that is in it, you islands, and all who live in them" (Isaiah 42: 9,10).*
>
> *"Behold, I will create new heavens and a new earth. The former things will not be remembered, nor will they come to mind. But be glad and rejoice forever in what I will create, for I will create Jerusalem to be a delight and its people a joy" (Isaiah 65:17,18).*
>
> *"The time is coming," declares the LORD, "when I will make a new covenant with the house of Israel and with the house of Judah" (Jeremiah 31:31).*
>
> *"Because of the LORD's great love we are not consumed, for his compassions never fail. They are new every morning; great is your faithfulness" (Lamentations 3:22,23).*
>
> *"I will give them an undivided heart and put a new spirit in them; I will remove from them their heart of stone and give them a heart of flesh" (Ezekiel 11:19).*

"I will give you a new heart and put a new spirit in you; I will remove from you your heart of stone and give you a heart of flesh" (Ezekiel 36:26).

"Forget the former things; do not dwell on the past. See, I am doing a new thing! Now it springs up; do you not perceive it? I am making a way in the desert and streams in the wasteland" (Isaiah 43:18,19).

So why do those of us in the church have such a hard time with change? It is because underneath it all we are human. We like familiarity, comfort, sameness, and consistency. Change produces stress, discomfort, and forces us to place our faith again and again in God versus traditions and habit patterns. New things keep us in tune with God, but old things allow us instead to trust memories and status quo. Even the best of us can be lulled into repeating yesterday's ritual instead of following the Holy Spirit to see if maybe, just maybe, He's taking a different path than the day before. The early founders of our movements were hardly men of tradition. John Wesley plowed a new furrow. Phineas Bresee was a spiritual entrepreneur, as were the other holiness founders. But like all organizations, secular or sacred, the tendency is to get organized, create structures and policies, and then to become institutional. The final result makes us unpliable and aloof to the world around us. Perpetuating yesterday's practices, which fail to be in tune with a changing society, will ultimately lead to our downfall.

Californians understand the mechanics of earthquakes, where two tectonic plates rub against each other, creating and releasing pressure which disrupts the lives of those nearby. We are in the midst of two paradigms colliding and pushing against each other. The new paradigm goes beyond new worship styles and seeker sensitivity. It has to do with how we think about and design ministry. The old paradigm allowed us to come up with a model of ministry which would work well for decades or even centuries, because society changed so slowly. But as the rate of change continues to escalate, a new paradigm, which allows for and promotes constant change and responsiveness to an ever-changing society, is emerging. The source of this new paradigm is none other than the Holy Spirit. The well-worn phrase applies here; we need to stop asking God to bless what we are doing and we need to start doing what He is blessing. The fastest growing evangelistic churches today are significantly different from the cookie cutter models of yesteryear. If we do not arouse our leaders to dream new dreams and promote an aggressive move toward entrepreneurism, we may as well turn our churches into holiness museums, in which we celebrate our wonder years and reminisce about the good ol' days. History is fine, so long as you don't live in it.

If we are to be effective in the future—no, today—we must understand that the ways of doing ministry have changed. Our culture is different. Our essence must never change, but to effectively communicate to the lost who are living in that contemporary culture, our form must always change. Jesus introduced a whole new spiritual paradigm, built on but going beyond the Old Testament scriptures and the Law. Wesley was ostracized because of his new message and new approach to ministry. Throughout history, people have stoned their prophets. It is a form of denial, pretending that if we just keep doing what we've always done, we'll be okay. Many of us have broken the second commandment by making our traditions our idols. Security is not found in well-worn and familiar music, in evangelistic or preaching styles. God is our comfort zone and He is dynamic, not static. He is ever on the move, creating new situations in which to trust Him and not the established way of doing things.

> *Then John's disciples came and asked him, "How is it that we and the Pharisees fast, but your disciples do not fast?"*
>
> *Jesus answered, "How can the guests of the bridegroom mourn while he is with them? The time will come when the bridegroom will be taken from them; then they will fast. No one sews a patch of unshrunk cloth on an old garment, for the patch will pull away from the garment, making the tear worse. Neither do men pour new wine into old wineskins. If they do, the skins will burst, the wine will run out and the wineskins will be ruined. No, they pour new wine into new wineskins, and both are preserved" (Matthew 9:14-17).*

New wineskins are needed to hold new wine. The question for most of our leaders and congregations is, "Are we still pliable enough to hold new wine?" If not, we should keep doing what we're doing and plan on dying with dignity. We must assertively be planting new wineskin congregations to make up for the pending death of hundreds and thousands of congregations in North America. Our hope is that many existing churches will be salvaged, transitioned to the new paradigm of ministry which is upon us.

The Writers

Joshua and Caleb were progressives. They spied out the Promised Land, recognized the giants, but focused on the milk and honey. They never doubted God's ability to provide for His people, to make a way in the wilderness. Progressives can scare people. They pioneer new trails and push people out of their comfort zones. As human nature goes, the Children of Israel chose to put their faith in the more cynical spies. Fear of the unknown rocked Israel's camp until they began murmuring about God and Moses. *What have they done to us? Look how good we had it back when!* Instead of seizing a challenge to enter a new territory, they chose to curse the opportunity, only to wander for forty years. Most of our churches do not have forty years to wander. Our members are graying.

This book is written by people in active ministry in various churches and institutions that are associated with John Wesley and the revival of the 1700s. Through the Wesleyan revival, God created organizations such as Methodism and others, which emphasized evangelical zeal, along with such biblical distinctions as the holiness doctrine. Like most denominations and church associations, those in the holiness movement— such as the Nazarenes, Church of God Anderson, Free Methodists, Wesleyans, Salvation Army and the like—are going through significant transitions in trying to relate to the changing world. Going beyond these individual circles of influence, we realize how much we have in common with others. Leaders in Baptist, Methodist, Presbyterian, Lutheran, Assembly of God, Catholic, Episcopalian, and countless other circles are going through comparable changes, striving to stay active and vibrant in the 21st century. God is definitely doing a new thing.

This book is specifically about the new thing He is doing in the North American church and what it looks like in various situations. The distinctions today are less doctrinal and more attitudinal. Churches which are growing and thriving today do so, not on doctrinal distinctions, but on mission orientation. Although denominational people would like to think such things as liturgy, tongues, eternal security or sanctification make us uniquely endowed to reach the lost around us, they are not. The paradigm difference has more to do with being purpose driven, mission oriented, and culturally relevant. No amount of doctrinal distinctions are going to save us. We are not suggesting that we drop these emphases if we believe they are a part of the niche we fill in God's Kingdom, but we are saying that to even preserve these in the next century, we must be about The New Thing.

The authors of this book are by choice in ministry associated with the Wesleyan holiness heritage. They realize that while ageless truths never

15

change, methods and styles do. Paul sought cultural relevance when he became all things to all people in order to win a few. Only a very small percentage of churches in our movement are experiencing significant growth, much less growth by evangelism. We play games with our words, suggesting that taking members in by profession of faith means evangelism, while most of our "professions of faith" are simply believers from other doctrinal flocks (i.e. Baptist, Methodist, etc.). Perhaps while emphasizing our second work of grace, we forgot sequence; that second and subsequent numbers are preceded by first. To get ahead we must get back to putting first things first.

In some ways, new paradigm leaders have more in common across denominational lines than with sister churches in the same movement who are not new paradigm in thinking. We may not say it often or loudly, but we feel it strongly. We sense it in district gatherings, when we read denominational materials, or when we discuss church matters. Just as churches usually split over philosophical and doctrinal differences in their approach to ministry, ministerial camaraderie flows along lines of mind-set more than doctrine. This affinity is hard to deny, but the growing awareness has caused some of us to bond together under a network called The New Thing (TNT). TNT is the name of a loose coalition of progressive leaders in the holiness movement, hosted by the Southwest Center for Leadership in Scottsdale, Arizona. These are people with an appreciation for retaining the distinctions articulated by John Wesley, but who also see the need to rearticulate these for cultural relevance. The goal of TNT is to network 200 of the progressive leaders in the Wesleyan heritage, to share ideas, encourage risk taking, and collaborate on resources. Our numerical goal is not lofty because we understand that progressives are always a minority, but the synergistic potential is tremendous. If you resonate with a majority of the ideas presented in this book, we encourage you to become a part of this network, designed to share ideas, sharpen one another with effective resources, link staff and address ministry needs.

Throughout the ages, God has always provided a few of His people with the unique ability to see over the next hill, to recognize the Promised Land when it is still a promise, and to declare it to those further back in the procession. The threshold of the 21st century seems a fitting time to gather a group of progressives, people who are gifted in detecting the future before it is fully upon us, who are willing to ride the crest over into tomorrow. These are the people who wrote this book. All are experts in their fields, ably equipped to show the rest of us where the church is headed in the next century.

The rest of us have a choice. We can repeat history, curse the predictions of the Promised Land, and suggest we go back to the "good old days." Unfortunately, like the Children of Israel, we won't and can't go back. The reality is that if we refuse to move forward, we will wander. Many churches are on the verge of death in the wilderness. While we move without progressing, a good number of us will die out and a new remnant will experience what we all could have seen, had we been willing to trust the two spies. History repeats itself because we stubbornly refuse to learn from it. Human nature never really changes, and so it is with a strange sense of *déjà vu* that we stand on the banks of another Jordan River . . . peering over its waters, straining to see if there really is any milk and honey on the other side.

Editor's Comment

These are indeed words of a transformational leader, perhaps even a radical. Words like these get people fired from institutional positions of ministry in our church. They are words not likely to get one elected to a role where political correctness is esteemed and "don't-rock-the-boat-itis" is the unwritten rule. The attitude is prophetic in nature. Change, transformational vs. evolutionary, is nearly always preceded by change agents who seem radical. "Those who emerge with new ideas, with new enthusiasm, or with new programs find they are blocked. Too many agencies are staffed with well-meaning managers or mean-spirited ideologues."[3] This is perhaps because progressives see a reality which these others do not. They yell, and scream, and wave their arms, shouting warnings of pending danger up ahead. But because the rest of the parade is not yet there, they are considered loose cannons and rebels. Sometimes only after their passing, by natural causes or stoning, are they recognized as correct, and sometimes even eulogized . . . post mortem.

These are my editorial words, not necessarily those of the other writers. Some of the authors sharing their hearts are indeed already in the Promised Land, shouting to the rest of us that there's nothing to fear. A few of the writers are precariously straddling both paradigms, the old and new. Their hearts are across the river, but their jobs and temperaments make them bridge builders between the progressives and slower adopters.

We are truly thankful for the host of witnesses who have gone on before us. We are all building upon the faith of our fathers/mothers and must never ridicule previous generations for doing their best in their times. But we must make sure that future generations will not criticize our integrity because we did not make the necessary changes when needed and were unwilling to leave our comfort zones.

Imagine a giant vessel from outer space, crash-landing in a community. Experts arrive, equipped with two-way radios. They spread out to observe the vessel from various angles because it is too large for one person to see completely. Each crew member describes what he sees according to his expertise and observation angle.

The church can be a big and complex system. The church of tomorrow is arriving today. The best way to read this book is in its entirety, because it was created as a collage and not as a collection of individualistic ideas. For example, you can read a lot of books on small groups or leadership, but how do these characteristics reflect The New Thing? By looking at and carefully contemplating the chapters of this book as a whole, you should catch the big picture of where we see the church headed. We try to avoid stylistic dating or models which are apt to go the way of passing fads. Rather, we strive to describe what we are seeing from different angles.

We use the phrases "new paradigm" and "21st century church" somewhat interchangeably, but we should note that "new paradigm" has more to do with new thinking and not so much with chronology. Many churches which are old in their thinking will exist in the 21st century, but their chances of being healthy and growing will be significantly reduced. When we use the phrase "21st century church or ministry," we are referring to those which are new in their thinking and more apt to display health and fruitfulness today and in the future.

This introduction aside, the goal of this book is not to criticize less progressive thinkers or predict gloom and doom if we do not intentionally, assertively make significant changes. The underlying danger of not making significant changes is very real. But the aim of the following chapters is to paint the picture of what ministry in the future will be like. Without appearing self-righteous, our goal is much like Joshua and Caleb's, to peek into the future and see wonderful things in store if we can just get across the river.

Welcome to future church. Those of us who wrote this believe you will enjoy your visit.

Alan Nelson
Scottsdale, Arizona
October 1998

ENDNOTES

[1]Mike Regele, *Death of the Church*, (Grand Rapids: Zondervan, 1995), pp. 184,185.
[2]Ibid., p. 198.
[3]Ibid., p. 208.

Chapter 1

New Paradigm Pastors

by Alan Nelson

*I*f you ask most people to describe a pastor, eventually the word "leader" will come up. In the broadest sense, pastors are leaders in that they are perceived as being in charge of leading, feeding, and serving people. In the literal use of the word, the pastor is not necessarily a leader. Most pastors are teachers, church managers, resident theologians, counselors, and nurturers. No one would suggest that these things in and of themselves are bad, but a new type of pastor is emerging. Much of the tension and burnout among clergy that is noted in the recent plethora of books, studies, and seminars is based on this silent change in the job description. We've recruited people who do not necessarily fit into the new position. The new role of the pastor is primarily that of leader.

Pastors, holiness or other, who will make it into the 21st century will need to retool, seek non-leading roles of ministry, or be resigned to diminishing fruitfulness compared with those more gifted in leading. We can curse it as a bait-and-switch situation, claiming that it's unfair to change the rule of the pastorate now that we have endured seminary, ordination, and perhaps passed up other careers. But with so many professions undergoing dramatic changes, we should not be surprised *that the pastorate is changing as well.*

Alan Nelson, contributing editor of this book, is somewhat of a pioneer in spirit. He is the founding and senior pastor of Scottsdale Family Church (Nazarene) in Arizona, which has grown from a core of 35 to over 700 active attendees in less than two years. His doctorate is in leadership from the University of San Diego and he is the author of books such as Leading Your Ministry (Abingdon), Broken In The Right Place (Thomas Nelson), Five Minute Ministry (Baker), co-author of The 5-Star Church (Regal) and numerous articles. Alan is also the founder/director of The Southwest Center for Leadership, of which the TNT network is a part. His passion for leadership development is seen in his writing and in his growing collection of over 350 books on the subject. He is married to Nancy and is dad to Jeffrey, Joshua, and Jesse.

Anyone who has purchased a car in the last couple of years knows that technology and enhanced design measures have significantly improved nearly all makes and models. One day, a parishioner allowed me to test-drive a very expensive BMW from his dealership. As we cruised down the road, we pulled alongside a "lesser" car, one which sported similar aerodynamic chassis lines. The dealer said, "It's a shame those cheaper cars look so much like these more expensive models."

Cars are just one of many things which have changed in recent years. Technology, politics, corporations, and social issues have seen numerous, significant changes. Although most pastors would acknowledge these and other changes among the congregations they pastor, few seem to seriously consider the idea that the role of pastoring is changing significantly as well. Pastors of the past were primarily shepherds, nurturers, church managers, counselors and teachers. They acted as the local priests of the temple, performing the sacred traditions of the church. But a different breed of pastor is needed in the 21st century. In response to the quantum changes taking place in society, today's need is for pastors who are primarily leaders.

The gifts, mind-set, and actions of leaders are quite different than those of the nurturing shepherd. The old paradigm pastor tends to be by nature a manager, one who tends to get involved in too many tasks. These take him away from what is most needed in the majority of churches seeking to grow in times of change . . . leading. Just because a man occupies the pastor's study does not make him a leader in the literal sense.

Leadership Journal illustrates the old paradigm because despite its numerous excellent ministry-related articles, few specifically deal with leading. The assumption is that pastors are leaders, regardless of whether they lead or not.

The typical pastor is one of the last few generalist professionals who perform a wide variety of tasks. Pastors teach, counsel, administrate, advertise, fund-raise, train, preach, and sometimes clean, construct, direct music, work with youth, or meet other specific ministry needs. Unfortunately, most pastors are not trained or developed as leaders. In many cases, they are not even wired to lead because the systems which recruited them have not rewarded leaders as much as they have good-hearted teachers and nurturers. A leader's job is to make sure nurturing takes place effectively in a church, but most leaders are not inherently nurturers.

The old paradigm basically sees the pastor as a hireling, a trained professional who performs a variety of ministries for the congregation and occasionally recruits a small percentage of others to help him do his job. When volunteers cannot be found, the congregation gives money to enlist the pastor and, if possible, a cadre of professional assistants to minister to and for the laity. As the church grows, so grows the number of tasks for the senior pastor. The number of hats increases, creating a tired minister and a frustrated congregation whose needs outweigh the capacities of even the finest of pastors. The result is clergy burnout, parishioner consternation, and typically a congregation which plateaus at or before the 250-member mark. This constitutes over 80% of American congregations.

It seems nearly everyone these days, within ministerial circles, is talking about the escalating burnout rate among clergy and the growing tensions in congregations. Books, seminars, pollsters, articles, and grapevine talk clearly show us that things are not as they once were in terms of pastors finding fulfillment with their work and congregations lovingly enveloping the care provided. The average pastoral stay per church is right at 3.5 years; the average career in ministry is 10.5 years. Why is this? What has changed in recent years to make the pastorate an unesteemed, draining career?

Have you ever tried to fix a machine when you needed a specific tool, say a screwdriver? Specifically, you need a flathead screwdriver but all you have is a Phillips. So you ridiculously try it but, of course, your attempt is futile. Next, you reach for a pair of pliers, thinking maybe you can grab the screw by the head and twist it out of the machine. No luck. Then you go to the junk drawer and scrounge around for a knife, a coin, or any other device that could possibly be forced into the gap to undo the screw. Your frustration grows with every unproductive attempt. Finally, knuckles bleeding, you run to the hardware store to buy the tool you need, or the machine remains unfixed.

Although a primitive illustration, a majority of our recent ministerial burnout and frustration levels are primarily caused by changing paradigms. We are caught without sufficient tools to deal with 21st-century ministry. We assume that if we just keep doing things the way we've always done them, with minor tweaks of the tools and systems, we will survive. Most people do not verbalize their growing frustrations, but the underlying awareness that things are not as they were is making us try to work with tools which just do not fit. Both clergy and laity are frustrated. We blame it on modern stress, the deterioration of the nuclear family, and any number of other more obvious symptoms, but the underlying problem is that the paradigms are colliding. "Church leaders work harder and harder, yet with diminishing returns. They tell us that for all their efforts, they realize they are losing ground. But on this model, no matter how hard one works, the gap is only going to widen."[1] Regele refers to philosopher Thomas Kuhn when he writes, "Paradigms start to falter when they begin to encounter anomalies. An anomaly occurs when we apply the paradigm's rules and procedures and find that we fail to accomplish the expected result."[2] A paradigm has to do with a worldview, a way to perceive and respond to reality, a mental model. Significant changes in life and church are creating a need for a new ministerial model but, unfortunately, many of us do not recognize this. So we do a slow burn as we try to fix our church problems with improvised tools.

Jethro ... Church Consultant

The way most of us have been trained to do ministry is not biblical. We can't really blame any one person or department. It is an evolutionary process down the wrong road, a road we've assumed to be right since others have sauntered its path. After all, how could so many sincere, godly people be incorrect? Seminaries are not the seat of the problem because they are primarily organizations produced by our past church cultures. Denominational leaders did not wake up one day and say, "Hey, the biblical model is not working the way we like. Let's try something else." The typical church model of ministry active the last century is a result of many preceding eras of incremental transition. Because none of us have lived long enough to see the significant changes, we base our experiences on what is around us. The present model is a natural emanation of godly men trying to do too much.

The present model has been glimpsed periodically through history. The earliest obvious example is Moses. In Exodus 18, Moses is suffering from near clergy burnout. There is no wonder why. He is trying to pastor over 1,000,000 parishioners, many of whom rise early to stand in line all day for a pastoral decision, judgment, or problem fixing. Moses' father-in-law shows up for what may be the first church consult. "What you are doing is not good. What you need to do is find those who will oversee 10, 50, 100, and 1000, and then you can handle the most difficult cases. With all due respect, Moses, you are not to be the do-it-all pastor. Your job is much more important than that. You are to be the developer of people. The people you are to develop must be gifted in varying levels of ministerial abilities. You need hands-on nurturers who can shepherd 10. You must find those who have managerial and shepherding gifts for 50. Then you must seek leaders (small l) who can oversee groups of 100, and superleaders (large Ls) who will supervise 1000. Each person has different gifts of varying capacities. Your job is to find and develop them. While you're doing this, there will probably be more, not fewer criticisms, because you will be stealing time from frontline ministry to invest in long-term staffing. The purpose is to improve long-term effectiveness. If you implode, no one is going to benefit and who will you have developed to take your place? For a while, you'll need to burn the candle at both ends, but then, you've been doing that anyway for short-term payoffs." As far as we know, there was no fee charged for this advice, since it came from a family member. Who knows, maybe Mrs. Moses put her dad up to it since she was fed up with not seeing her husband. Regardless, the wisdom was divine and remains just as potent today.

The problem with many of us who have a concern for people and who are called to full-time service to Christians, is that we find too much pleasure in frontline ministry instead of building organizations made up of frontline ministers. We should not be shocked by the idea that we've taken the wrong path in recent decades, perhaps even centuries. Moses, the man who met with God, one-on-one, needed some outside ideas. God could just as well use Moses' father-in-law as He could a staff, a burning bush, or a pillar of smoke. We should not be surprised that so many well-meaning mentors and institutions of our past have emphasized improper ministerial roles. But that does not mean that we should perpetuate the situation. It is not chance that in the next chapter of Exodus, God tells Moses to inform the people that they are to be a nation of priests. "All

Israel is going to present me to the world, so start seeing yourselves as pastors, all of you, not just the Levites." The New Testament equivalent is 1 Peter 2:5,9 where we are reminded that we are a holy nation. If we are going to adopt the new pastoral paradigm, which is really the old one, we need to cast the vision to our people that they must fulfill their roles as ministers.

> *"It was he who gave some to be apostles, some to be prophets, some to be evangelists, and some to be pastors and teachers, to prepare God's people for works of service, so that the body of Christ may be built up until we all reach unity in the faith and in the knowledge of the Son of God and become mature, attaining to the whole measure of the fullness of Christ. Then we will no longer be infants, tossed back and forth by the waves, and blown here and there by every wind of teaching and by the cunning and craftiness of men in their deceitful scheming"* *(Ephesians 4:11-14 NIV).*

The role of teachers, pastors, and leaders is to equip the believers "for works of service." Until we get the leaders doing their jobs, we'll not be unleashing the laity to serve, and we won't be helping our people mature. If I always do the work for my kids, they won't develop as they should. For too long, pastors have been doing far too many ministry tasks for the congregation. Then we wonder why we are frustrated because there are so many immature believers in our midst.

So, do we abdicate God's work? Don't people need pastoral care? The pastor's job is to make sure ministry takes place, but not necessarily perform the ministry himself. When the Early Church needed people to care for the widows, the leaders did not say, "Hey, we're busy. The widows can take care of themselves." Rather they said, "The widows need to be cared for, but we must be about our work as well." Then they discovered and unleashed those who would provide the personal touch. The problem is that those able to do a specific ministry must be found and developed by others who may *not* be able to do that ministry.

Why The Change?

When you are recruited and hired to do one job and then someone changes the job description in the middle of your career, it doesn't seem fair. But that's exactly what's happening in the church.

Unfortunately, it is not the result of a malicious or even wishy-washy board. It is evidence of a strong, underlying, cultural transition which seeks pastors who are wired and trained to lead over more traditional teaching, caring, managing types. We cannot be certain why the pastoral paradigm is changing, but we need not look far to get some pretty good ideas.

1. *Lay Movement.* As never before, laity are rising up. They are disgruntled with the thought of sitting passively and allowing a few trained professionals enjoy all the action. Part of this is Holy Spirit induced. People active in ministry demonstrate a church's vitality, health and growth. This is seen in a resurgence of contemporary evangelism, such as that of the seeker-sensitive and Willow Creek movements, and in an emphasis on spirituality and holiness, as seen in the Promise Keeper mega-rallies. Dissatisfied with the nine to five rat race, people are searching for deeper meaning in life. Certainly all church attendees are not active in ministry, but a growing number want to find a place of significance in serving others. This requires a pastor with a leadership orientation to develop and unleash the church. Filling slots is the old paradigm concept of lay ministry. Just looking for enough teachers, ushers, or board members to vote is becoming a dinosaur mind-set. Don't recruit. Invite people to participate in ministry for the sake of their own soul's growth. Ministry is a service we provide for people, whether it is inside or outside the official church programs. Spiritual gifts assessments, lay ministry resources, and developmental tools are all signs that God is helping people catch the vision for lay ministry.

2. *Boomers & Busters.* It is not by chance that the paradigm shift is taking place during a time when the Boomer generation is reaching mid-life. This generation, different from any previous one, has brought widespread change to numerous people movements. The articles and books written on the subject are legion. Needless to say, Boomers have always been activists. From their teen and college years of war rebellion and drug experimentation, they have wanted to change things, to challenge the norm. Perhaps the Holy Spirit is at work today because the conditions are ripe for change. The Baby Boomers are aging and with their emergence into the mid-life mode, there is a kinder, gentler, and less materialistic Boomer mind-set. The "been-there-done-that-now-what?" syndrome has created a critical mass of people interested in the deeper issues of life. Since Boomers have always been pro-participation—from

the anti-war, love and drug-fest rallies of the 60s, to the do-it-yourself orientation of the 70s and beyond—we want to get involved when we go to church. Our musical style engages more of our senses, with toe-tapping, rock beat worship styles. That mentality carries over into ministry, in that we want to experience our religion and not just watch it from the back pew. Unfortunately, the old paradigm (where a few professionals get the pleasure of serving others) does not allow for widespread participation. Although simplistic in its theme, the underlying cultural differences in this generation have made it easier for the Holy Spirit to do a new thing in lay involvement, requiring those of us in pastoral ministries to equip and unleash people for ministry involvement. Since we cannot do our old job and new job with quality, we must invest more of our time in the new job. Research shows that GenXers are even more adamant about putting feet to their faith.

The Boomers and Busters are also the best-educated generations in history. Typically, as education increases, so does the desire to participate and lead. In the "good old days," pastors were often the best educated and the tendency was to manage in a factory-foreman manner. A growing percentage of professionals in the pews means that we are less able to manage as we have in the past. Many of our people are better educated and handling faster and larger careers than those of us in the pastor's study. This means that our managerial style has to change as well. Sharper people seek to be well led, not poorly led or managed. The greatest unused asset sits in our church audiences every Sunday. Millions of dollars flow to parachurch and social organizations because we are not providing significant enough vision for our parishioners locally. The people want to be led and led well, but what many of us provide instead is a pastor who represents our kind Uncle Ted and not a leader with a prophetic vision to attack the gates of hell.

3. *Larger Churches and Complex Ministries.* With the rise of social complexity and such realities as dysfunctional families, we see a growing need for diverse ministries, specifically designed to solve certain issues. With Boomers being the first generation to be raised on shopping malls and a postwar capitalistic craze, we are consumer oriented. Small churches do not have the resources to respond to a large array of emotional, social and spiritual needs. Thus, people band together in larger groups, pooling resources often known as megachurches. One out of every seven churches nationwide accounts for 50% of the total attendance.

Although maintenance of a large church does not require leading per se, to grow a large church does require leading. Churches with the vision to keep growing require leaders. The large church movement is more leader intensive than the churches of 200 members and below.

4. *Social Rate of Change Escalating.* Society is changing more rapidly than at any other time in history. Mergers, takeovers, transfers, and technological revolution have created career uncertainty, economic imbalance and resultant emotional distress. Change creates stress and stress is the number one health hazard today. Leaders are needed during times of change. They help us make sense of it, respond to it with a positive attitude and align us to it. People dealing with perpetual change during the week look for leaders inside and outside the church who will cast the vision and provide the direction desired. They look to pastors for guidance as leaders, not just counselors or spiritual technicians. They want to be told what this change means, how they are to respond, and how they can maintain hope in these times.

5. *Holy Spirit Revival for Post-Modern Times.* Many churches and denominations in America have moved beyond inception and high-growth phases into institutional, maintenance cycles, preparing for the decline phase. Some of the mainline denominations are already in the decline phase. This is typical of nearly all organizations, not just churches. Unless there is renewal, the movement will cease. Jesus talked about the need for new wineskins to hold new wine. God is seeking to do something new in our nation. This is not apt to take place in the old wineskins, whose unresponsiveness to change makes them vulnerable to rupture. Churches across America are bursting as they work through transition, many unsuccessfully. "That's not the way we did it before." "If it's good enough for my parents, it's good enough for my children." Phrases such as these reflect old wineskins. New wineskins almost always require leaders to envision them and make them happen. Leaders deal with change. The Holy Spirit may be getting the church ready for unprecedented growth in the coming years. To do this means we must develop leaders and not managers; prophets not priests.

Soul Inc.

While the 19th and 20th century models for ministry sought pastors who were primarily nurturers and feeders, the emerging 21st century model pastor is more a CEO of a spiritual corporation. Those from the traditional paradigm loathe to even consider such a concept, but I think there are several reasons why this metaphor is a good one.

Certainly some of my biases are based on my education. After getting a solid biblical literature degree from Olivet Nazarene University, I did not sense God leading me to seminary study, even though that was a traditional next step. Since most of my work would involve communicating, I did not feel further study in similar subjects would be as productive as a broader look at communication and psychology. One of the best in my state was California State University in Sacramento. While in my first senior pastorate, a church plant in southern California, I realized my greatest need was not for more theology or language study or even traditional church-growth concepts, but for leadership training. Already gifted in this area, I wanted to understand the concept more deeply and broadly, so I pursued a doctorate at the University of San Diego, a Catholic institution. I share this personal background so that you may understand why I believe so strongly that we need a different mind-set in ministry.

There is a risk of becoming entrenched in our traditions and mental models, so that we reproduce methods which are not healthy and/or which do not allow us to create vital ministries. Traditionally, our denominations have elevated men from within who work the system, but who also perpetuate the same old ways of ministry. There is a benefit to considering other forms of ministry, especially if they are succeeding. I was raised in various Baptist churches, an Assembly of God church, and then Nazarene and Wesleyan congregations. I am a part of the holiness movement by choice, not because of tradition or because I know no other way. Through my writing and teachings, I try to experience both secular and broader Christian circles, allowing at least a glimpse of life beyond the holiness movement.

With over 350 books on leadership in my growing collection, I note that the best and brightest thinkers in the field are predominantly corporate. Business generates money and, therefore, tends to gather those who seek the cutting-edge. Leadership, however, is a somewhat generic subject, especially the emerging 21st century paradigm. This type of leading is much more servant-like, focusing on team building and avoiding the Great Man theory which can still be seen in many corporations and churches. Unfortunately, business zeal so often outshines spiritual zeal. If we took our work as seriously as many business leaders, we would aggressively seek innovation, implement new ideas, and pursue change with a do-or-die attitude. Anyone in the corporate world knows that if you don't stay on or near the cutting-edge, you run the risk of extinction.

For the most part, our churches lack this zeal, which is why so many are becoming endangered species. Leaders are those who catalyze change and pursue necessary course deviations to reach the destination. We need men and women who have the minds of priests, but the souls of prophets. This kind of catalyst understands priestly duties but also transforms sleeping congregations into frontline teams, struggling for their very existence. People are going to hell. Eternities are being determined while we sing one more hymn and endure one more boring sermon. In our churches are business leaders who wouldn't even consider doing the things we are doing in the business realm. You say, but we're not in business, we're the church. That's part of the problem. We think of ourselves more like family and this keeps us from developing need-filling ministries, aggressive marketing (I mean evangelism) and top-quality service.

We are a business. We're in the business of helping people grow their souls. And, yes, our "product" is really a service—but so are a majority of American corporations today. We are competing with other agencies which strive to entertain people, consume their money, and care for their children. Only we have the best product available to help people nurture their most important aspects, their spirits. That product, of course, is Christianity, a personal relationship with Jesus Christ. Other religions claim they have the answers, but we do not believe they do. We do. And everyone we meet desperately needs the services we make available to them. The local church is the key to Kingdom building. Parachurch ministries are wonderful, but they are not the same. God has chosen the church to perform His work. We are all local franchise operators.

To be a corporate CEO does not mean one becomes sterile or impersonal. We teach our people that they must be holy in all they do, secular or sacred. We are not more holy just because our work is in the church. Many corporations have an incredible sense of community. There, friendships blossom and people are excited to be a part of the mission. Some are far healthier than many of our churches. We do not have to give up our bent on spirituality, character growth, community and love to think of ourselves as spiritual business leaders. But doing this helps us break out of the confining mental model of what a shepherd is and does that diverts our movement from its destiny. We must consume cutting-edge thinking from the fields of business and leadership, spit out

31

the secular, and translate the truth to unleash our congregations. Innovate, market, and plan strategically as if your life depends on it, because the eternities of many do. If something doesn't work, toss it. Move on to something else. Cast a vision. Align resources. Help people of influence know your heart. What is your passion? What will catch your church on fire? What is your niche? How are you different than XYZ church? Read. Grow. But don't bury yourself in the same old pastoral model of yesteryear because yesteryear can only be seen in the cemetery. Move the gospel of Christ into today and tomorrow.

Transformational Leaders

The kind of leaders we need in the 21st century church are primarily transformational rather than incremental. We must be about aggressive church planting, but the temperament necessary to start a church is unique. Entrepreneurial gifts and innovative, resilient character are a must. Far too few churches are being planted to keep us from plummeting over the pending precipice of so many dying congregations. Besides that, the attrition rate for church starts is far too high, due primarily to lack of visionary leadership. We will need to find and develop risk takers and give them permission to take chances. It is one thing to give permission, and quite another to fund this risk. Twice I have talked to district officials after sensing God was leading us to start a church, and twice my wife and I were turned down. In one case we switched to a sister denomination. In another we left for another district. Denominational officials must be willing to grant permission to risk takers who possess the character and initiative to start new ventures. There are no guarantees. The only certainty is that if we do not begin new ministries and pioneer new ideas, we will go the way of the stagecoach and eight-track tape player.

The second arena in which we need transformational leaders is in the realm of church transitioning. There are nearly 300,000 congregations in America and over 85% of them are plateaued or declining. Only 1% of churches are growing due to seeker, unchurched evangelism. There will be a need for thousands of pastors with visionary ability to take existing congregations and help them make the transition to the future. Besides having significant wisdom in political environments, the leader must exude vision and boldness.

Because some people have had a bad experience with ineffective, "bold" leaders, they have a misconception of what constitutes a strong leader. Ineffective leaders can be like the proverbial bull in the china closet, who crash and burn while striving to make significant change in a church. This is not an indictment against strong leadership, but rather emphasizes the need to better train leaders in effectiveness. People want to be a part of a well-led organization, one in which there is teamwork, excitement, motivation, purpose, vision and community. But what pastoral leadership most lacks these days is passion. A vision is a dream with passion. Without passion, a vision cannot excite. With no dream, passion becomes oozy sentimentality. The issue is not "either/or" but "both/and."

"The transformational paradigm does not assume personal survival but instead vision realization at any cost. If the vision lives and thrives, it does not matter if the leader is fired, assassinated, or humiliated. The vision itself is far more important than personal survival."[3] This is the kind of prophetic demeanor which is required by those of us who want to see a new dream conceived in our congregations. Too many of us care too much about being accepted or not rocking the boat or not offending donors or becoming an ecclesiastical ladder climber. Compromisers don't lead transformational organizations because they are unwilling to put the dream before their own careers and reputations.

Seminal Seminaries

The problem is the proverbial catch-22. The old system tends to recruit people who are managerial and shepherding nurturers by nature. Leaders tend to be removed or overlooked in the process. The church culture selects those who are more diplomatic and willing to do what it takes to fit into the corporation, those who are not apt to create many waves. Unfortunately, we are not attracting leaders. Churches complain to seminaries that they are not producing the sort of graduates who are ready to pastor 21st century churches. Seminaries counter-complain to churches for not sending them healthier, more leader-like candidates for full-time ministry preparation. It's a systems problem. The system recruits those who fit the old paradigm pastorate. We will not be able to develop leader-pastors until we develop systems which seek and recruit those with leader gifts. Leaders are both made and born. The Bible teaches that we all have certain gifts and that some are gifted as leaders. Although many people can learn leadership principles, only a minority will ever display the gift. All we need is a minority, however, because leadership in essence has to do with a few influencing the many. But when very few leaders are being developed as pastors, we have little hope that the future will change in favor of leader-pastors.

The role of the pastor is to be a local seminary to train and equip people for ministry. This means that the role of the seminary is to prepare pastors to think and act like leaders and trainers. During my dissertation research, I looked at 141 ministerial preparation programs in evangelical North America. My search was for programs focused on teaching and training students in the area of leadership. My hypothesis—that hardly anyone was teaching leadership with any significance—was validated. The last part of my dissertation involved developing an optimum training program for pastors. It looked something like this:

- Theological Education: Some criticize theological school reformers because they fear we will lose the essence of homiletics, hermeneutics, the languages and systematic theology. We must have these basic tools to avoid ignorance and heretical teaching, but developing the basic tools and helping students become lifelong learners are sufficient. We often answer questions that no one is asking.

- Practical Theology: Recent reform has helped us work on our practical theology, namely pastoral counseling, church administration, and similar tools. Practical theology is best learned on the job. Classroom pastoral preparation is a relatively new phenomenon. Historical preparation was done almost solely via mentoring and living with and around a chosen teacher. Jesus' style for ministerial preparation was hands on, day in and day out activity, modeling, debriefing, delegating, teaching. To be potent, practical theology must move toward effective internships.

- Leadership: Leadership needs to be a core subject for new paradigm pastors. They need to know the elements of leading, social dynamics, people skills, social psychology, and they need hands-on mentoring and personal analysis with 360 degree instruments. We can never assume someone knows how to lead because we ordain them or grant them a degree. Principles such as vision casting, change, influence resources, and training are essential for 21st century leaders.

- Spiritual Formation: A part of the mentoring and leadership development process involves the character development of the pastor himself. We must move toward living out what we teach before we preach. We cannot assume at any time—and especially dysfunctional times—that because a person claims a call, he or she has the character traits required of Christian leaders. Teaching spiritual attitudes and disciplines, such as integrity, character issues, self-denial and self-discipline must be an integral part of pastoral development. Again, classroom study is a start but most of this comes through ongoing discipleship by spiritual mentors.

So, why don't seminaries jump on this sort of 21st century program? I've passed on similar ideas to seminary staff with the promise of further discussion, only to never hear from them again. The primary reason I was told it wouldn't work is because of turf. No professor wants to give up any of his turf for something new. They don't want to cut back the languages or systematic theology to make room for leadership studies. They can't just tag on more classes because they would lose students due to time and cost. Therefore, it's not apt to happen until the pain becomes acute. When their student populations decrease to the point that finances deplete, then they will consider change. Growing numbers of institutions are hurting, but the few who respond to this positively and proactively will emerge the leaders in the 21st century. Institutions such as Bethel and Golden Gate Seminaries appear to be leading the way, as this book goes to press. Others which show signs of renaissance are Denver, Asbury, Azusa Pacific and Regent Universities. Cavalier groups like Campus Crusade are charting new models of ministerial preparation, at least abroad, and the Willow Creek Association is striving to build alliances with seminaries to renovate the system.

The 21st century began to arrive in the early 90s. The pastorate, as is true of many other vocations, is not apt to be what it was in the past. The future will be left to those of faith who run the risk of appearing foolish, who daunt status quo, and who rely on the fresh movement of the Spirit to go beyond the Jordan one more time.

ENDNOTES

[1]Regele, *Death of the Church*, p. 196.
[2]Ibid., p. 192.
[3]Robert E. Quinn, *Deep Change: Discovering the Leader Within* (San Francisco: Jossey-Bass Publishers, 1996), p. 124.

Chapter 2

Exploding the Lay Ministry Myths

by Gary Morsch and Eddy Hall

*G*ary Morsch and a covey of people like him are like surfers on the crest of a big wave that keeps building. The lay movement, unlike anything we have seen in history, is looming on the horizon. Whether this is due to boomers hitting mid-life and seeking something more, or the cultural search for what is real—a search for high touch in a high-tech world—or an anointing of the Holy Spirit, or a combination of these factors, it is a reality that lay ministry is on the rise. I shudder at even the mention of the term, lay ministry, because ministry is ministry, regardless of who does it. For too long we have adopted the unbiblical model of the clergy doing ministry for and to the laity. We must move toward the biblical model in which the professional staff is committed to helping develop and deploy the lay staff. Moses did it. Jesus did it. Martin Luther spoke of it, but we must begin seeing all believers as ministers, as priests, and we must unleash them.

*This movement is not sequestered in holiness or evangelical circles. It is being felt in mainline, Catholic, and charismatic circles. The New Thing is that lay ministry is no longer a way to recruit new church workers, to fill empty slots in ministry flow charts. Rather, ministry is a natural expression of who we are in Christ, allowing us to grow spiritually as we help others grow. Each of us must find our unique calling and respond in obedience. Pastors must quit doing ministry **for** people and begin working **through** them to expand the Kingdom. This requires special gift mixes and skill sets than traditional pastoral roles. We must also help believers understand that their calling is not just a role within the narrow boundaries of the local church. In essence, they are to be Christ's ambassadors in the schools, offices, malls, fraternal organizations and neighborhoods where much of ministry takes place.*

Two great men to bring us these ideas are Dr. Gary Morsch and Eddy Hall. Gary is a physician with an incredible energy level, creative mind, and humble spirit. He refers to his medical practice as his tentmaking ministry which allows him to invest time in broader ministries. He is the founder and leader of Heart to Heart as well as the Center for Lay Ministry (Nazarene). Gary is the author of various works, but most recently The Lay Ministry Revolution *(Baker), from which this chapter is an excerpt.*

Eddy Hall of Goessel, Kansas, is a church planning consultant who helps congregations maximize their ministries through integrated planning of ministries, staffing, facilities, and finances.

In the 1950s, Elton Trueblood wrote, "If the average church should suddenly take seriously the notion that every laymember—man or woman—is really a minister of Christ, we could have something like a revolution in a very short time."[1] Today growing numbers of churches are experiencing this revolution. But in most churches, most members still don't see themselves as ministers. As a result, church staff are overburdened while many members feel sidelined.

What is keeping Trueblood's revolution from sweeping through all our churches? For centuries, the church has divided Christians into two distinct groups—the ministers (clergy) and those ministered to (laity). This division has been maintained by the perpetuation of four *ministry myths*—unbiblical beliefs about ministry that have shaped how most Christians approach ministry. The revolution will come to your church when these four ministry myths are exposed and members act on the biblical truths that these myths have so long obscured.

MYTH 1: Ministry is just for "ministers."

God calls certain people to church leadership, and their role is essential. But, in describing the call of leaders, Scripture doesn't single them out as the "ministers." Rather, it emphasizes the ministry of all believers: "The gifts he gave were that some would be apostles, some prophets, some evangelists, some pastors and teachers, *to equip the saints for the work of ministry"* (Eph. 4:11-12, NRSV, emphasis added).

Gordon Cosby, pastor of the Church of the Saviour in Washington, D.C., says it this way: "The primary task of the professional minister [is] training nonprofessional ministers for their ministry."[2]

Our friend Mark knew that all Christians were called to minister, but he bought into the version of this myth that says that God can *best* use those in professional ministry. Wanting God's best, he quit his job, earned a seminary degree, then joined a church staff where he was responsible to coordinate the ministries of others.

In his new job, Mark quickly discovered that his gift was not administration. "I'm most effective in one-on-one ministry," he explains. "And rather than coordinating existing ministries, I'd rather be bringing new people in. I thought joining a church staff would give me more time for these things, but in fact it limited how much time I could spend doing what I do best."

Mark resigned from the church staff and went into insurance even though he knew some people would think he was settling for "God's second best."

"Though I didn't realize it when I started," Mark says, "insurance is a perfect job for someone who wants to work with hurting people. Whenever a client loses a spouse, I get a phone call. When any of my clients divorce, they have to come to me to change their insurance papers. And, of course, whenever one of them has a car accident, a fire, or a serious illness covered by insurance, the client comes to see me. Just a few weeks ago I told my wife that I've never before felt God using me in ministry like I have lately."

This ministry myth led Mark into a church staff job that actually hindered his freedom to minister. Only when he understood that God could use him more effectively in the business world was God able to put Mark's ministry gifts to fullest use.

MYTH 2: Ministry refers only to meeting spiritual needs.

When I (Eddy) was in college, sometimes on Sunday afternoons I would go to a park with a few friends and we would approach strangers with *The Four Spiritual Laws*, a booklet that explained how to become a Christian. A half dozen or so of the people I talked to prayed the sinner's prayer. One even came to church afterward for a few months.

In time, however, I grew uneasy with this cold-turkey witnessing. For one thing, I saw little evidence that it was leading to changed lives. But part of my discomfort, I believe, also stemmed from my own changing relationship with God. Nurtured by my pastor's sermons, I was seeing God less as a critical judge—making a list and checking it twice—and more as a loving Father. I was beginning to realize that God was not only concerned about my getting to heaven; He also cared about my joys and pains, my hopes and fears. He was willing to guide me, provide for me, strengthen me, and comfort me. God didn't care only about my soul; He cared about me.

The more I experienced God's love, the clearer it became that I was not treating the people in the park the way God treated me. I was treating them as objects, as trophies to be won, not as people to be loved.

Somehow, early on, I had gotten the idea that ministry involved meeting only—or at least primarily—spiritual needs. Witnessing, preaching, teaching the Bible, leading worship—this was ministry. But feeding the hungry? Visiting the sick? They were all nice things to do, I would have told you, but hardly ministry.

But as love replaced law as my motivation for ministry, I started seeing other people through new eyes. I became less concerned with persuading others to do the right thing and more concerned with helping them. Ministry, I realized, had to be concerned not just with spiritual needs, but with the needs of the whole person. Love can't limit itself to caring about one kind of need.

When people believe ministry is restricted to meeting spiritual needs, the people God has called to meet physical or social needs may end up feeling like they have no ministry. When this myth is exploded, these people can find their places in the body of Christ.

MYTH 3: Most ministry takes place when the church is gathered.

If you asked a group of people in your church to list your church's ministries, how many of the first dozen or so answers would be activities that take place in the church building? In a typical church, about ten are on-campus ministries.

Most Christians, when they think of ministry, think first of what happens when the church is gathered. But that is exactly backwards. Most ministry is to take place when the church is scattered.

In some ways the church is like a sales team. When the team meets, its members may celebrate accomplishments. Sales managers may inspire and motivate the team, give them a vision of what is possible, and provide training. Group members may encourage one another or empathize with each other's problems.

Now what would you think of that sales team if, upon leaving the meeting, the members made little or no effort to sell? Would you suspect they missed the point of the meeting?

We in the church are not a sales team but a ministry team, yet we gather for many of the same reasons—to celebrate, to expand our vision, to be inspired to fulfill our mission, to give and receive encouragement, and to become equipped for ministry. If then, at the end of our gathering, we go out into the world but make little attempt to minister, what does that suggest?

If, upon leaving church on Sunday, we don't go out into the world to minister as the church scattered the rest of the week, we've missed the point. As one pastor says, "The church is most the church when the sanctuary is empty."[3]

MYTH 4: Some Christians are called to do secular work.

Jan Lundy runs a ministry organization, but you won't find it listed in the Yellow Pages under that heading. You'll have to look under "Laboratories." Her business, Precision Histology, is a medical laboratory in Oklahoma City which prepares microscope slides of tissues from which doctors diagnose patients' illnesses.

As the world measures success, Precision Histology has not made much of a splash. For the first few years Jan had to reinvest all her earnings into the company to buy equipment. Today she earns only a modest wage. But that's okay with Jan, because Precision Histology is succeeding at what it was created to do.

"From the beginning, our main purpose has been to help people," Jan explains. This happens in various ways. Jan hired lab technicians with little technical skill and gave them on-the-job training. Often these were mothers from low-income families who lacked the resources to pay for formal training. One technician she hired was already trained but was recovering from drug addiction and was not physically able to go back to work in the hospital. Jan made it possible for employees to keep their children with them at work by providing a play area and, when necessary, hiring a child-care worker at no cost to the mothers.

The lab has prepared slides at no charge for three local nonprofit clinics serving low-income patients. But, at its most basic, the lab ministers through the services it is paid to provide. As the company name implies, Jan insists upon work of the highest quality. "I treat each slide as though it is for a member of my own family," Jan says. "After all, each one is for *somebody's* mother, brother, or sister. Doctors need to be able to interpret slides easily and accurately. If my slides enable them to do that, I am ministering to the patients whether they know it or not."

The world says there are two kinds of work—sacred and secular. The dictionary defines secular as "not holy" or "not sacred." But the Bible tells us that we are to do everything—even eating and drinking—to the glory of God (1 Cor. 10:31). For the Christian, every activity is to be sacred.

If God directs someone to be an auto mechanic, it is because God can better use that person to meet needs as an auto mechanic than as a pastor or missionary. Every Christian is called to full-time Christian ministry. Any Christian can transform a legitimate "secular" job into a ministry by approaching that job with a commitment to meeting people's needs as an expression of God's love. If a job cannot be performed as a ministry, a Christian has no business doing it.

God doesn't call anyone to do "secular" (unholy) work. He calls us all to bring honor to God and to minister to people's needs through whatever work we do.

Ready to Join?

Once our understanding of ministry is broad enough, we can then discover which particular part of Christ's mission God is calling us to do. Two invaluable clues to call upon are pain and joy.

PAIN: Where do you mourn with Jesus for the pain in the world?

JOY: What would bring you joy in that painful situation?

When you can answer those questions, you have probably found your call. As Frederick Buechner says, "The place God calls you to is where your deep gladness and the world's deep hunger meet."[4]

Once the church explodes these four ministry myths, helps members identify their calls to ministry, then supports them in creatively fulfilling those calls, we will, as Trueblood predicted, experience something like a revolution in a very short time.

The revolution is underway. Is your church ready to join?

This chapter is adapted with permission from THE LAY MINISTRY REVOLUTION: How You Can Join *by Eddy Hall and Gary Morsch (Baker Book House, 1995). Designed as a catalyst for congregation-wide renewal, the book includes a study/action guide with step-by-step instructions for six training sessions.*

ENDNOTES

[1]Elton Trueblood, *Your Other Vocation* (New York: Harper & Brothers, 1952), p. 9.

[2]Quoted in Elizabeth O'Connor, *Call to Commitment* (New York: Harper & Row, 1985), pp. 40-41.

[3]James Garlow, *Partners in Ministry*, videorecording.

[4]Frederick Buechner, *Wishful Thinking: A Theological ABC* (New York: Harper & Row, 1973), p. 95.

Chapter 3

Staffing the 21st Century Church

by Alan E. Nelson

I *periodically attend forums sponsored by Leadership Network. Most of the people attending these events are denominational leaders, consultants, pastors and staff members from churches averaging 1000 and above. In some of these discussion groups, the average church size is 3000. Nearly every time leaders at this level gather for informal talk on their ministries, the most common topic arising has to do with staff challenges. As with any industry, it just seems tough to find and keep good help. With the number of large churches increasing, the need for more effective staffing will increase. It is estimated that a church of 1000 is added every week in America. Whereas the multichurch staff used to be somewhat unique, it is now commonplace. While staff challenges are a perpetual problem in large churches, a growing number of middle-sized and smaller congregations are also involved with staffing, both professionals and lay.*

If senior pastors harbor frustrations regarding staff competency, attitude, loyalty, and hiring and firing, a popular theme among staff discussions is finding a great senior pastor and team to join. As one frustrated staff member said, "All senior pastors are b_ _ _ heads!" When I quoted this staffer in a recent Leadership Network group I attended, the senior pastors roared with laughter. They humbly recognized it must be frustrating from both sides of the staff team. All of this is to say that how we relate to staff is changing, as is the rest of our ministry. Having listened to frustrated leaders and staffers, experienced both sides of team roles, and read a growing body of literature which has to do with team play, I've drawn some conclusions about how staffs work in The New Thing.

Seven trends characterize the new paradigm style of staffing churches.

1. Raising Homegrown Staff: With the rise of the lay movement and the need for more staff in larger churches, a natural response has been to employ qualified lay people to grow into ministry roles. There are several benefits to this. The upside and downside of homegrown staff are listed and explained later in this chapter.

2. Staff as Leaders: The old paradigm sought staff who could "do" effective ministry. With the rise of the lay movement and the need for greater people development, staff must not only know how to "do" a specific ministry, but must be able to develop teams of people to perform ministry tasks. For example, we used to look for a youth pastor who would work with the youth. Now we need a person who understands youth culture and ministry, but whose primary task is to develop adults to work with youth. This requires an additional and more sophisticated skill set than doing youth ministry alone. The downside of this is that there are fewer people who can handle both tasks. The upside is that a person who *can* handle both tasks will cause less disruption to the ministry if he leaves, because he has built a team of mobilized youth ministers to carry on the youth ministry. We must find people who will help us minister to ourselves rather than merely provide ministry *for* us.

3. Better Pay and Resources: Because of culture and competition, church leaders and boards must pay more attention to mundane items such as salary packages and staff resources than we have in the past. Too often we have taken advantage of staffers with inadequate pay and miserly support, and then been astonished at their short tenures. The move of the future is to find top-quality people and then care for them well. This is not just in terms of salary, health, and retirement benefits, but also in professional resources. It is difficult to keep a staff person stimulated when there is no budget for ministry events, training, and resources. It is a shame to hire a sharp person, only to tie his/her hands for lack of resources to create innovative ministry. Wages and raises should be based on performance, improvement, and market demand. Some people are more difficult to replace than others and should be compensated for appropriately.

4. Perpetual Training: As the times change and organizations grow, there is a need for continual training and staff development. Peter Senge of MIT (The Fifth Discipline) coined the term, "the learning organization." For churches to keep learning and growing, they must be led by staff who are learning and growing. Perpetual training can be done in weekly staff meetings by providing leader lessons, articles, video clips, and by bringing in resource people to provide short, focused ideas to educate and stimulate staff. Making learning a consistent part of staff meetings also models for them what they are to be doing for their ministry teams. Training is expensive. Many companies spend 5-20% of their budgets on training and development. Churches have been notorious for throwing a manual or assignment at a person and not providing the tools needed to effectively carry out the task. Sending people to conferences, subscribing to periodicals and tapes, and promoting continuing education will be the trend in cutting-edge ministries.

Just as organizations change, people must change. Although the goal is for long-term staff commitments, we must be honest and suggest that all ministry is seasonal. There is a time and place for everything. A staff member might be right for a certain season of a church or ministry, but when that seasons changes, he or she may not be right. We must communicate from the beginning that the goal of the leader is to be committed to helping the staff member grow, but that we all have limitations and capacities (i.e. parable of the talents). If the person is not able to grow with the ministry, that person's rightness for the season of the ministry may be over. The same is true of pastors. Church boards must lovingly call the hard shots in helping develop a pastor and, if necessary, find a new pastor for the next season. No one person is more important than God's dream for a church. By understanding the philosophy of growth and rightness, you can hopefully communicate the importance for personal growth and avoid some hard feelings when a transition is necessary.

5. Obfuscation of Paid Vs. Volunteer Staff: Another dynamic that a rising lay movement is creating is a diminishing demarcation between professional and volunteer staff. The whole concept of "lay" ministry is antiquated, because ministry is ministry regardless of who does it. Pastors must see that their staffs include paid professionals as well as part-time and full-time volunteers. (Ten ways to do this are included later in this chapter.)

6. Team Building: The primary role of the pastor in new paradigm church staffs is to build team spirit and nurture a culture where we thrive on growth and ministry. Past pastoral paradigms have been managerial in their approach, governing over staff members like foremen in a factory. This autocratic, top-down, boss type mentality has diminished team spirit and created a division between pastors and "hirelings." The new paradigm sees pastors as player/coaches who are teammates themselves. They include fun times in team building, mutual brainstorming, relationship building, and people development. Too many pastors hide in their studies, pushing papers or preparing sermons instead of interacting with staff members, building morale, doing quality control, motivating, and encouraging. Team builders are less likely to have staff problems and even when they must say farewell to members, the members do not feel betrayed in the process. Too many spineless seniors have resorted to unloving, ungodly terminations, simply because they lacked the quality people skills needed to work with staffs. Churches must not behave like their secular counterparts, who often treat employees like inanimate assets. Team building has to do with individual and team development in order to maximize ministry effectiveness.

7. Pastors as Leaders/Vision Casters: Just as the pastoral paradigm is changing, so is the leadership paradigm. Leaders in the future are kinder, gentler, and more team oriented than in the past. They realize their job is to create synergy among the many parts, not just "lord over" an organization. To be a 21st century leader requires greater people skills and organizational savvy. The greatest need in the church is for men and women of vision and passion to catalyze our churches and seize the opportunities around them. What worked yesterday is not working today. What works today will not work tomorrow. Leaders help us with change. They give us a sense of confidence that we can enter the Promised Land and defeat the giants who would keep us out. Churches and staff love to be well led. The whole concept of team building, developing lay and professional staff, ongoing training, and staff care tends to be a leadership issue. Everything does not rise and fall on leadership as some would suggest. Life is too complex for such a simple explanation. But a lot does rise and fall on leaders. Staffing in the future is going to be more and more important as we prepare for larger and more flexible ministries than ever before.

(The following section first appeared in *Vital Ministry*, Jan-Feb, 1998 edition)

Homegrown Staff

Recently I heard about a church which laid off five professional staff and hired support staff for twelve volunteer ministry directors. There is a fading delineation between professional and nonprofessional staff, both paid and volunteer. A growing practice is to grow your own staff. Several influences are creating this trend, such as the burgeoning lay movement, decreasing budgets, larger ministries which are better at developing staff members via training and modeling, a growing frustration with seminary preparation, and a number of negative experiences with outside clerical staff. Professionals need not respond defensively to this trend as an anti-clergy movement, but rather should see professionals and laity, paid and voluntary staff, as fellow team members.

The old paradigm suggests that only those who have seminary training and a call as a young person to full-time Christian service are proper for official church staff status, excluding administrative and janitorial support. The new paradigm suggests that biblical and/or seminary training is a plus for senior pastors, but what qualifies other staff members is the demonstration of giftedness, loyalty, enthusiasm for a ministry area and leadership. The latter is a prerequisite because the goal is not to hire ministers but to recruit those who can train and develop laity to minister. This requires a different set of gifts than that of traditional ministry. The "call" can be in the traditional form of sensing God's leading to full-time Christian service. It can also be the confirmation of the body (staff and lay) inviting the person into a staff role.

Benefits of Homegrown Staff

1. *Perhaps the strongest reason for elevating lay people to staff status is that they are raised in an environment where they understand and are committed to the philosophy of ministry created by the pastoral staff.* Too often we assume that schisms arise because of doctrinal differences, but philosophical discrepancies create more tensions than theological ones. Professional staff from different backgrounds may not buy into the cultural and ministerial culture of the church. People raised in the culture of the local church are more apt to believe in, think and act to perpetuate the values of that unique ministry.

2. *Prior to inviting a lay person to staff level, you have the opportunity to observe the person's temperament, loyalty, ministry and work ethic.* The New Testament church elevated ministers who were recognized by the congregation as people with character and ability. Many of us have been burned by glowing but incomplete recommendations on professionals. You are not always sure of outsiders until you have hired them and can observe them in action. How does the person respond under pressure? Will he be loyal to me? What is his energy level? Is she teachable? Is the person a *prima donna* or a team player? The answers to these questions are difficult to ascertain before hiring a professional and only become clear through experience.

3. *Hiring lay people is often more economical.* Some can work for free or at a reduced salary, based on their financial status. We should not assume that unless we pay someone he/she will not be committed or loyal, and that we cannot develop or fire them. This has more to do with treating them as any other staff member, which will be discussed later. Some lay people will donate numerous hours as long as they have support staff and a budget, which is less investment than paying a professional staff salary. You can more often begin lay people on a part-time basis than you can bringing in a professional, allowing the part-timer to earn their keep as their ministry grows. You also save on relocation costs.

4. *Homegrown staff tend to be more committed to long-term ministry because they are less interested in seeing ministry roles as stepping stones.* Their interests are less self-directed and they are more committed to investing in their community than an outsider might be. The idea comes from Jesus' story of hirelings who run from the flock when the wolf attacks. The stimulus for a professional to leave might be a wolf (tough time) or a more attractive offer from a larger flock.

5. *Homegrown staff come with an existing local network of friends, neighbors, and contacts, both inside and outside the church.* There is always a learning curve and time of adjustment for professionals. Given the short average tenure of staff (6 to 36 months, depending on the position), this leaves little quality ministry time after one has acclimated to a new church and community.

How to Treat Volunteers Like Paid Professionals:

Pastors who want their volunteers and part-timers to behave like staff members need to consider how they treat staff. Volunteers can usually detect walls between them and the "real" staff. Tokenistic inclusivity can sometimes compound the feeling of being "just a volunteer." If you are serious about tearing down the barriers between paid and volunteer, professional and lay staff, here are ten workable ideas.

1. *Include all those you consider staff in staff meetings.* Naturally, you may need to schedule meetings on evenings or weekends for those who work others jobs. Our church has a bimonthly Ministry Leadership Team (MLT) meeting, consisting of all ministry directors, paid and volunteer. These people are responsible for the ongoing, viable ministries in our church. Because of the growth, we do most personal sharing in small groups, but we mail ministry reports of praises, progress, and needs prior to the meeting so everyone can be updated and have the opportunity to network before and after the meeting. MLT is used for team building, leadership training, calendar announcements, and fellowship. I meet at least monthly with key ministry directors who oversee strategic ministries and as needed with others. I meet weekly with program staff who create and carry out the Sunday morning and midweek worship services.

2. *Train, train, train.* Training and education are among the most effective ways to help staff feel like staff, because you are investing in them. Take them to ministry conferences. Send them to formal and informal learning opportunities. Invest in their education as professional ministers, whether paid or volunteer.

3. *Give them your home phone, private e-mail address, pager or cell phone numbers.* This communicates that you consider their roles important and you esteem them by providing them with access to you. If you give this information to everyone, it will not be as esteeming, but consider providing staff with more personalized time with you. Return their calls first and right away.

4. *Hold them accountable.* Provide a written job description and use it. Although accountability at times means confrontation, this is a genuine characteristic of good staff relationships. Just because a person is a volunteer does not mean that he or she should not be held responsible for commitments made to ministry and excellence. Confrontation needs to be done positively and with love. Sometimes the best way to know you've made the "inner circle" is if you are expected to be accountable and to act like a staff member, whether you are paid or not.

5. *Provide a budget and expect periodic progress and feedback reports.* Giving budget allotments is a significant way to communicate value and position to volunteer and part-time staff. Along with ministry money comes the stewardship of financial accountability and progress reports on what is happening—good, bad and indifferent. Feedback is what the staff can expect from you. How do you think they are doing? What would you like to see from them in their ministry area? How do they think you are doing as a staff developer and leader?

6. *Include all the staff in an annual retreat where you team build, plan, brainstorm, and set the course for the upcoming year.* Take time to hear their goals, struggles, and accomplishments. Celebrate with them. Cry with them. Pray with them.

7. *Equip them.* If facility space is not a problem, provide an office or even a cubicle where staff can prepare for their ministry. Being around other staff members accentuates the sense of inclusion. If facilities do not

provide for individual office space, then invest in other resources such as administrative support staff, home office equipment, stationery, stamps, and a key to the office. More and more companies are helping employees cocoon at home. Recently, our church purchased a computer, fax, pager and cell phone for a volunteer to work from a home office.

8. *Provide nonverbal perks and titles.* Talk about various staff and their ministries in messages and newsletters. Have a commissioning service annually for all ministry staff. Publish their pictures in brochures. By including them with the paid professional staff, you level the playing field. In our church, we list all ministry directors with their phone numbers on the back of our worship folder so that people know who to contact (thus reducing church office calls), and holding the people listed accountable. Give them business cards with their names and ministry title. We do distinguish ordained staff from others with the title "pastor," but that is about the only distinction we make. Have staff participate in services, praying, making announcements, or interviewing a worker in their ministry area.

9. *Don't do their job for them.* When you put people in charge of a certain ministry area, let them do it. This does not mean you dump it, never check in, or do not provide for support and accountability. It does mean you equip and motivate them to do what they can do best. When you have an idea or see a need pertaining to their area of ministry, always work with and through them. When you make decisions over their heads, their sense of importance is diminished. Pulling rank is a common temptation for professionals because working with and through people takes more time and effort, but remember, you are developing people, not just programs. Take the time to meet with specific staff to discuss problems, ideas, and strategic tasks which you believe fit in the overall vision for the church.

10. *Refer others to staff members.* When someone asks you about a certain program or ministry which comes under another person, avoid answering it for them. Refer the person to the staff member and/or ask the staff member to follow up on the issue. By resisting the urge to be the answer person, you elevate the status of the staff member and also unload some of your burdens. When a person has an idea or a complaint, ask if he has shared it with the staff member. If not, then suggest he do that first and then talk to you about it. You diminish the importance of staff

members when you talk or act for them.

Some of your finest future staff members are probably right under your nose.

Potential Shortcomings of Homegrown Staff

Naturally, there are some potential shortcomings with establishing lay people as staff members, which is why some leaders are nervous about such promotions.

1. *The most obvious drawback is a lack of professional training.* Churches require those who administer the sacraments to meet various qualifications, but few staff roles require meeting these kinds of qualifications. Most lay people who have received sufficient spiritual discipleship can obtain the necessary initial and continuing education to direct a ministry. For example, a children's director can take local college courses in early childhood development, attend children's ministry conferences/workshops, read related books, and mentor under a neighboring children's minister.

2. *Lack of respect and local baggage.* All of us carry a certain amount of baggage which hinders our ministry potential. An outsider tends to start with a clean slate, but in a few months, he will tend to have accumulated his own baggage. More difficult to overcome can be the "prophet in his hometown" syndrome. When a person who is raised in a local church becomes a staff member, some parishioners can balk because they knew him/her when he/she was "just a layman." A person who has not earned the respect of others likely should not be elevated to a staff role to begin with, since the best call is the affirmation of the body.

3. *Difficult to confront/fire.* Because a homegrown staff has a local network of friends and family, it can be more difficult to confront or fire a local staffer. Even more difficult is a volunteer. This is usually not a problem because you tend to hire better when you have seen a person in action. When you establish an official relationship with a staff person, you are very up-front about the working relationship, the criteria for reward, and your expectations.

4. *Tunnel vision.* Many universities will not hire their own alumni as professors in order to continually broaden the teaching philosophies of

the faculty. Homegrown talent can become inbred and tunnel visioned. When a lay person only knows one way of doing church, this can create boxed-in thinking. The way to avoid this is to continually introduce your staff to new models, books, tapes, and conferences for the purpose of expanding the vision in that ministry area.

Staff Infection

While there is no such thing as a perfect pastor or staff member, we can hopefully avoid some common problems. Following is a list of the seven most common staff problems. This was originally published in one of Alan's columns for Vital Ministries *magazine.*

You can't live with them. You can't live without them. Staff. That's what we all feel from time to time as leaders, whether working with volunteers, paid or not. When we grieve over staff problems, chances are we fell short in one or more of these areas.

1. *Haste Makes Waste:* The discomfort of a vacancy is far less painful than hiring the wrong person. Wait for the right person. Think of hiring a staff member as more like a marriage than the purchase of a new car. You don't propose to a person you've only dated once. Consider worst case scenarios, dilute glowing recommendations from references, and take time to sleep on it without stringing a candidate along insensitively.

2. *Focus On Task:* Strategic thinking looks for key roles where people are needed and recruits according to strengths. It does not build a position around a favorite person. If you hire the right person for the wrong position, you're risking disaster. We all hate to see a plum staffer slip by, but if the person does not fit the role you need to fill, you've been a poor steward of resources and will later regret hiring that person.

3. *Know Your Faults:* Many leaders are natural at selling a dream and seeing the best in people, but those are not always the best skills for hiring someone. Seek an experienced person in human relations or someone deeply discerning to recommend potential staff. A number of leaders I've talked to tend to be overly optimistic and sometimes don't ask the tough questions when interviewing. Because leaders

are positive, they are sometimes blindsided by assuming everything will work out. As in marriage, minor differences in dating tend to become chasms after the honeymoon.

4. *Hire For Attitude:* You can often teach skills, but rarely can you teach attitude or character. Agreeing in philosophy of ministry is more important than doctrines and theology. Attitude makes the person livable as a team and family member. Since our work mandates a certain caliber of attitude, talented staffers with bad attitudes are automatic liabilities.

5. *We're All Temps:* Avoid firing by communicating from the start that we're all temporaries who are right for certain seasons of organizational growth. *Everything is beautiful in its time.* When that season has passed, affirm the person but acknowledge the need to move on. You can be loving and still confront the reality that a staff person has outlived his or her effectiveness. A leader is responsible for helping a staff member develop his/her potential, but know that everyone has capacities (i.e., one, two, or five talents, as the parable explains). Most staff need to be measured in three areas: talent, attitude, and organizational skills. A person who plateaus in any one of these areas will tend to become a liability, even if he overcompensates temporarily in another area. Peter Drucker said that for every 20-30% of growth, you need to restructure an organization. During these times, staff either rise to the occasion or let it be known that they cannot change adequately enough to take the ministry to the next level. Do not confuse love and acceptance of staff with avoiding the tough decisions which, if not dealt with promptly, can hurt the organization. By the way, church boards need to do the same with pastors as well.

6. *Avoid Clones:* Diversity helps us avoid blind spots. When two people think identically on a matter, one is not necessary. Consider differences in temperament and strengths as a plus, while differences in attitude and philosophy of ministry are a minus. Weak leaders are threatened by differing opinions and strong staff. Strong leaders revel in diversity.

7. *Leadership Reflection:* If you find perpetual staff frustration, share the blame and analyze yourself, because staff reflects leadership.

Strong leaders hire/recruit strong staff. Weak leaders either do not recruit or do not keep strong staff. I'm amazed how certain church leaders process staff like a meat grinder, always blaming them as unmotivated and incompetent. Others tend to hire those who never threaten them and thus rarely hit homers, because they cannot handle strong staffers. Just as we tend to marry according to our self-esteem, we tend to hire staff according to our self-image as well. Strong egos are not necessarily big egos. The former build great, even if imperfect teams. The latter fail to draw or even retain winners.

(Vital Ministries, March-April, 1998)

Chapter 4

Turning Church Committees into Ministry Action Teams

by Stan Toler

*E*ver attend a boring committee meeting or wonder why in the world you were spending your free night off, micromanaging ministry minutia? The old paradigm is set up to elect or appoint people to committees, which are an organizational evolution based on somewhat static, maintenance-oriented cultures. During times of change and leadership paradigms, teams are needed to fulfill tasks and engage people into action-oriented relationships. The difference is more than semantics. Teams have different DNA than their forefathers, committees. You can play games with the names, but know that unless you intentionally design your task-

oriented groups to function as teams, you're probably going to end up with a committee.

Teams tend to build around tasks and gifts rather than checks, balances and positions. They are usually more relational in their processing, bent toward making changes as needed. Committees are more oriented toward membership and making recommendations. Teams tend to be more short-term, based on the task at hand. Committees tend to endure longer and sometimes continue with little respect to the task at hand. Although these are conveniently exaggerated, the seemingly small differences spell major differences in the outcomes they produce. There is nothing wrong with committees in a managerial culture. As we have discussed, the new paradigm is predominantly leadership-oriented, and therefore requires new structures such as teams. Teams tend to require and develop leaders who work with managers to accomplish the task at hand.

Stan Toler is one of those guys who is bridging the two paradigms. His experience has taken him through times of traditional ministries, but his networking and forward thinking is helping us make the transition to the 21st century. Stan is the senior pastor of Trinity Church of the Nazarene in Oklahoma City, Oklahoma. He is incredibly busy with other ministries, such as hosting the NCN program, "Leadership Today," teaching the Model Church Seminar for InJoy, and authoring/co-authoring numerous books and resources such as You know You Might Be A Preacher If, God Has Never Failed Me, But He's Scared Me To Death A Few Times, The People Principle, *and* The Minister's Little Devotional Book. *He is currently co-authoring a book on quality with Alan Nelson (Regal, 1999 release). Stan plays tennis when he isn't being a husband and dad.*

I love the story about the two men who were riding a bicycle built for two. It seems that everything was going well until they started up a rather large hill and then the struggle ensued. When they reached the top, the man on the first seat was gasping for breath. He looked back at his partner and said, "That hill took a lot out of me!" The man in the second seat said, "You're right, if I hadn't kept the brakes on all the way we would have rolled back down the hill!" Perhaps this delightful story gives us an insight into the world of church committee meetings!

A study of 341 pastors in 36 different denominations revealed that unrealistic expectations from church committees were a major source of frustration to most pastors. H.B. London, Jr. recently stated, "Most pastors are chronically fatigued!" London cited the primary reason for fatigue as pastors spending most of their time caring for their flocks. Could it be that part of this frustration revolves around the fact that church leaders spend long hours in committee meetings dealing with a "brakes-on mentality"?

What on Earth Does a Church Committee Do?

Have you ever wondered, "What on earth does a church committee do?" I have! After pastoring for nearly thirty years, I have discovered that most church committees focus on the following areas in order to maintain the status quo:

1. Planning the church calendar
2. Dealing with personnel matters
3. Spending and budgeting finances
4. Maintaining and expanding facilities

Unfortunately, very little time is given in most committee meetings to vision casting, strategic planning or evangelism and discipleship. In fact, as a church gets larger, it becomes increasingly more difficult to become proactive in these vital areas of ministry. Why? Because the pastor and any formally paid staff members are caught up in facilitating traditional programming.

Churches usually grow to the energy level of the senior pastor. When the pastor runs out of steam, the church loses any momentum that has been built. Often, this results in discouragement and low morale in the church. In a nutshell, that is why I turned to ministry action teams.

Why Build Ministry Action Teams?

Someone has said, "Every team needs a leader!" How true! I would add, "Every leader needs a team!" To grow the church, pastors and lay leaders must learn to involve the church membership in team ministry. As Jim Garlow says, "Every member must understand that they are built for ministry!"

Why have a ministry action team? The answer is found in the word "action." It indicates that something might be accomplished! I recommend empowered ministry action teams for the following reasons:

1. Shared Vision and Values. Every ministry action team needs to understand Matthew 28:19-20 - *"Therefore go and make disciples of all nations, baptizing them in the name of the Father and of the Son and of the Holy Spirit, and teaching them to obey everything I have commanded you. And surely I am with you always, to the very end of the age."* Church teams must fulfill the mission of Jesus and understand the value system of a holiness Christian!

2. Biblical Models for Team-Building. In Acts 6:1-8 we read, *"In those days when the number of disciples was increasing, the Grecian Jews among them complained against the Hebraic Jews because their widows were being overlooked in the daily distribution of food. So the Twelve gathered all the disciples together and said, 'It would not be right for us to neglect the ministry of the word of God in order to wait on tables. Brothers, choose seven men from among you who are known to be full of the Spirit and wisdom. We will turn this responsibility over to them and will give our attention to prayer and the ministry of the word.' This proposal pleased the whole group. They chose Stephen, a man full of faith and of the Holy Spirit; also Philip, Procorus, Nicanor, Timon, Parmenas, and Nicolas from Antioch, a convert to Judaism. They presented these men to the apostles, who prayed and laid their hands on them. So the word of God spread. The number of disciples in Jerusalem increased rapidly, and a large number of priests became obedient to the faith. Now Stephen, a man full of God's grace and power, did great wonders and miraculous signs among the people."* It is quite obvious from reading this passage that the early church leaders understood team building and sought out team members who could save them from the "if-you-want-things-done-right-do-it-yourself" syndrome.

The writer in Romans 12:4-5 emphasized the importance of team building with the following analogy, *"Just as each of us has one body with many members, and these do not all have the same function, so in Christ we who are many form one body, and each member belongs to all the others."*

The natural world gives several examples of shared leadership. Engineers have used wind tunnels to calibrate why flocks of geese always fly in the "V" formation. They discovered that each goose, when flapping its wings, creates lift for the bird flying next to it in formation. The entire flock gains more than 70 percent greater flying range than one goose flying alone. From time to time, the lead goose falls back from the point position and another assumes the lead without breaking the formation. Every goose takes the lead during long migratory flights. Each contributes his or her unique talents to the overall effectiveness of the flock. It should also be noted that the geese who are following honk to encourage the one leading.

3. Increased Effectiveness. One of the most prolific passages in Scripture, Ecclesiastes 4:9-10, warrants a careful study of church leaders. *"Two are better than one, because they have a good return for their work: If one falls down, his friend can help him up. But pity the man who falls and has no one to help him up!"* Once I discovered the joy of team building, I was delivered from those lonely feelings of "Who pastors the pastor?"

Defining Ministry Action Teams

Definition: A ministry action team is a group of church leaders working together for the common purpose of building God's Kingdom.

In order for this to be accomplished, every church needs a clearly defined mission statement. One of the first things that I have tried to do since accepting my pastoral assignment at Trinity Church of the Nazarene is to facilitate the creation of a mission statement for the church body.

Perhaps the following example will clarify my reasons for anchoring everything at Trinity to the following ministry statement.

The Mission and Vision Statement

The focus of our mission is to know Christ and to make Him known to others. Commitment to that mission will give purpose to our ministries. As we come to know Him, we are changed to be more like Him. Our vision is to be a church of and for FRIENDS:

F ocus on Relationships
R enew our Commitment
I nvite to Participate
E quip to Minister
N etwork the Body
D emonstrate God's Love
S erve with Gladness

Therefore, every ministry team leader and every ministry action team is asked to base every decision they make on the mission/vision statement of Trinity. Thus, our statement becomes the glue that holds everything together in each ministry of the local church!

Every great team has clear job descriptions for its team members. As a part of my organizational process at Trinity, I met with every existing committee and chairperson and sought understanding as to their role in the church. With the help of Pastor Jeffrey Johnson, I then attempted to bring role definition and team understanding into sharp focus.

We began redefining the role of the Church Board. My first goal was to move us from dealing with "nickel and dime" issues to becoming a vision planning team.

The Ministry Vision Team

The purpose of this team is to give direction to the life and ministry of this church toward the accomplishment of the church's mission as stated.

Accomplishing this purpose will involve:

- Developing and maintaining a strong, well-balanced and inspirational church program which ministers to the needs of every age group, so that all may grow and mature in discipleship.
- Developing and maintaining a definite program which involves our people in the outreach of the church. Doing so will require that we provide training, assistance, and direction as necessary for maximum effectiveness.
- Obtaining and maintaining facilities which are functional in nature, adequate in size and equipped with sufficient equipment.
- Developing and maintaining a program of financial support that is strong enough to underwrite these programs and facilities.

Organization of the Ministry Vision Team

To assure that positive attention is given to each of these areas, this team shall be organized as follows:

1. Sixteen team (church board) members and three ex-officio members.
2. The three ex-officio members are Missions Team Leader, Youth Team Leader, and the Sunday School Superintendent.
3. The team will elect corporate officers within the team by a ballot vote. These elected officers will serve as secretary and treasurer.

4. The board members will be appointed to serve in one of seven areas of ministry. The seven areas of ministry are:
    a. Fellowship
    b. Stewardship
    c. Worship
    d. Friendship
    e. Partnership
    f. Leadership
    g. Discipleship
5. The three auxiliary officers and departments (youth, missions and Sunday School) will be structured according to church manual requirements.

Responsibilities of the Ministry Vision Team

- Team members are limited to a maximum of three consecutive one-year terms of service.
- Team members must rotate off the Ministry Vision Team for one year. It is expected that individuals leaving the team will be involved in subcommittee work.
- The three-year tenure also includes the ex-officio members (youth team leader, missions team leader, and Sunday School superintendent).
- The Ministry Vision Team will meet monthly to hear reports, review minutes, conduct an annual audit, study statistics, review plans and take appropriate action for the general operation of the church. Attendance at each monthly meeting is expected.

One assignment that I disliked the most in church work was being the "chairman of the church board!" I have never enjoyed chairing meetings. Frankly, I talk too much to be a chairman and I must confess that I have prostituted the chair by doing so! Further, I was "thin-skinned" when church board members would go off on a topic and express criticism. I just didn't deal with it well. Often I carried the critical comments home and laid awake until the wee hours of the morning. Finally, I resolved the matter. First, I came to the realization that people were not criticizing me in the board meetings; they were actually trying to deal with areas of church ministry that needed help and cared enough to point them out. Secondly, I decided that a lay person chairing the meetings could "take the heat" better than I could and to my surprise, most board members were "kinder" and "gentler" to their peers. What a discovery!

With the new understanding that I didn't have to chair all the meetings, nor be present for all the meetings (I do make most of the board meetings), I felt a sense of release to do ministry and to fulfill my best "gifts" more than ever before!

I would hasten to point out that I have an important role in the church board meeting, which we now call Ministry Vision Team meeting. My role is to cast the vision. Therefore, I try never to get caught up in the mundane matters. Rather, I am there to lead the church board to a new level of ministry.

Now that I have mentioned the use of a board president, I would like to describe the role of this ministry action team leader. The following job description has been written for this important team leader at Trinity:

Ministry Vision Team President

The Ministry Vision Team President:

1. Will serve as Ministry Vision Team Leader. This office will be for a one-year term of service.
2. Will guide the agenda for each Ministry Vision Team meeting.
3. Will serve as assistant to the pastor on the Executive Ministry Team.
4. Will prepare the agenda for the Ministry Vision Team meeting as a result of the Executive Ministry Team meeting, with the approval of the senior pastor and with consultation for additional action items. Will submit to the church office for typing.
5. Will assist the senior pastor in watch care of the staff and their families.
6. Will spend quality time in encouragement of the overseers and their various committees.
7. Will sign documents, checks and other church papers as appropriate.
8. Will call Ministry Vision Team meetings with the approval of the senior pastor and/or district superintendent, in the absence of the senior pastor. No Ministry Vision Team meeting will be called without such approval.
9. Will chair any specially called corporate officer meetings. Meetings are to be called with the approval of the senior pastor and, whenever possible, at a time the senior pastor can

attend. Senior pastor is ex-officio chairperson of all boards and committees of the local church.

10. Will assist the pastor with the affairs and activities of the church with love and loyalty for all.

Ministry Action Team Leaders

Since I have established a team leader for the church board, the next important issue is the employment of ministry team leaders. These individuals are appointed by the senior pastor and head up the seven vital areas of the church that were mentioned earlier in this chapter. After many meetings in the study committees at Trinity, we were able to develop the following job description for our team leaders:

1. Ministry Action Team Leaders will be appointed by the pastor. This appointment will be for a one-year term of service.
2. Ministry Action Team Leaders can be appointed for more than one year, but they cannot lead the same team for two consecutive years. (This does not include the Stewardship team.)
3. Each team leader will make a monthly report to the Executive Ministry Team and to the Ministry Vision Team.
4. Each team leader is responsible for submitting any expenditure that needs additional approval to the Executive Ministry Team.
5. Monthly committee information submitted by the team leaders will form the completed agenda for the next Ministry Vision Team meeting.
6. Team leaders should meet monthly with their teammates. Never conduct a meaningless meeting—cancel the meeting if there is no reason for meeting.

Ministry Action Teams

Earlier I stated, "Every leader needs a team."

1. Each team will consist of a leader and at least two members.
2. Each team is expected to meet once a month. The leader is responsible for communicating the time, date, and place of each meeting.

3. Each team will have financial guidelines (recommended by the Stewardship Ministry Action Team and ratified by the Ministry Vision Team) that entitles each team to make financial decisions independent of Ministry Vision Team approval.

4. Each team will have a financial ceiling cap that will require certain expenditures to be approved by the Executive Ministry Team.

5. Each team is responsible to involve non-board members and church attendees to serve on ministry teams.

6. The auxiliary committees (Youth, missions and Sunday school) are to be structured according to manual requirements. Each of these auxiliary presidents and superintendents will be assigned a Ministry Action Team Leader to assist them in ministry when needed.

The goal is involvement. I often tell staff members, "I measure the success of events, etc. by the number of people you involve in the process."

Since I have been discussing ministry in general terms, the following example of our Stewardship Ministry Action Team may provide additional insight.

Stewardship Ministry Action Team Purpose:

1. To direct the development of an effective stewardship program in order to assure adequate funds to meet the budget needs of the church.

2. To supervise the proper handling and disbursement of such funds.

Responsibilities:

1. To study financial standing and needs of this church and to recommend a long-range financial plan to the Ministry Vision Team.

2. To plan periodic stewardship emphases for the membership of the church and to make recommendations regarding same to the Ministry Vision Team.

3. To establish a priority for the outstanding financial obligations of the church and to make recommendations regarding same to the Ministry Vision Team.

4. To nominate, for Ministry Vision Team approval, a Counting Ministry Team and chairperson who will be responsible for the counting, security, and deposit of all church receipts.
5. To nominate, for Ministry Vision Team approval, a Financial Records Secretary who will be responsible for the maintenance of individual contribution records.
6. To arrange for an annual audit of the financial records of the treasurer, Youth Ministry, Sunday School Ministries, and any other financial records of the church.

Guiding Question:

How can we assure that the church will have access to the facilities and finances it needs to meet its commitment to our congregation and our community?

The Pastoral Staff Team

Nearly every church that has over 150 in church attendance employs at least one full-time staff person.

I am often asked, "Where does the paid staff fit into all of this?" The answer is simple. They are part of the church ministry team and must learn to work with ministry action team leaders. I do not have room for "lone ranger" types on the team. Every staff member matches up with a team leader and is asked to resource and encourage the lay ministers with whom they work. The following job description for the pastoral team has provided guidance for the "paid" leadership team at Trinity:

- The senior pastor and staff will meet weekly in a regular session to deal with spiritual and administrative matters of the church.
- The staff will work with the appropriate Ministry Action Team Leaders to facilitate their individual ministries.
- The Executive Ministry Team and Ministry Action Teams are to work with the staff to facilitate the ministries of the staff as well.
- The staff will make any financial request that needs additional approval to their Ministry Action Team Leader. The team leader is responsible for taking this matter to the appropriate team or the Executive Ministry Team if needed.

- The pastor maintains full responsibility of the staff and their own individual ministries. The Ministry Action Team Leaders' involvement does not override the pastor's responsibility for the staff.

Obviously, the paid staff must model team work and accountability for the lay ministry teams. The design of the above ministry description reflects the desire to work together with the church team leaders.

While it is impossible to describe every ministry team in this brief chapter, the following grid clearly delineates the variety of ministry areas of the local church:

Seven Ships of Trinity

Leadership	Partnership	Friendship	Discipleship	Fellowship	Worship	Stewardship
•Vision Casting •Preaching •Mentoring Leaders •Lay Institute to Equip •Evangelism Training •Leadership Training	•Lay Ministry •Structure for Ministry and Growth •Building and Properties ▴Maintenance ▴Security ▴Equipment ▴Vehicles ▴Improvements	•Friendship Evangelism ▴Prayer ▴Encouragement ▴Evangelism/ Outreach •Unchurched Events •Hospitality ▴Pastors Brunch •Athletics •Weddings/ Showers •Wednesday Suppers	•Guest Welcome/ Follow-up •New Member Assimilation •Pastor's Welcome Class •Gift Discovery Class •Discipleship Classes	•Sunday School Ministries ▴Children ▴Youth ▴Adult ▴Sr. Adult (SAM) •Women's Ministries •Men's Ministries •NWMS •NYI •Small Groups	•Worship Services •Music •Celebrations •Baptism •Special Services •Communion •Audio Visual •Decorations	•Advertisement/ Community Relations •Budget Preparation Regulation & Review •Records & Reporting •Auditory •Stewardship Emphasis •Fundraising •Business Operations •Money Counting Team •Financial Contributions Secretary

So what's the bottom line? Our Trinity Ships sail smoothly when our Ministry Teammates have clearly defined roles and job descriptions. Empowered leaders with clear understandings assist greatly in Kingdom-building!

Chapter 5

Relevancy Bytes

by Wes Dupin

*W*hen I get together with my peers at district events, sometimes
I take a little razzing for not wearing socks with my
Topsiders or for wearing t-shirts with jackets or golf shirts
instead of suits and ties. My goal is not to be intentionally
rebellious or out of sync, but I do not think of myself as a
typical pastor. I am a suburban missionary to the lost of north Scottsdale.
I dress and drive and eat and live pretty much like the people to whom
God has called me to minister. More and more, if we are to be effective
in reaching the lost around us, we must quit thinking of ourselves as
traditional church pastors and more like missionaries. We don't make fun
of African missionaries who give talks in their indigenous garb. In
America, we no longer live in a Christian society but in one which is post-
Christian in its mentality. This affects how we conduct our business, the
communication forms we use, the ministry tools we incorporate, and the
way we relate to people. Jesus, Paul and the great missionaries
throughout history have tried to bridge the gulf that exists between
cultures. What does Jesus look and sound like in my culture? If you
haven't noticed, there is a pretty large chasm between traditional Sunday
morning services and the Monday through Saturday society.

The holiness in our heritage might tempt us to shrink from
evangelistic attack, circle the wagons and hold on for dear life. The result
would be an Amish-like existence—with holy demeanor, but very weak
evangelism. The New Thing God is doing is stretching us to become all

things to all people in order to win a few. Instead of bashing the local idols, we, like Paul, are more apt to talk about the shrine to the unknown God. Jesus was incredibly effective at employing liberal methodologies to communicate with people, while never compromising His standards. That is the call for holiness churches in the 21st century, to stay our course in godliness, but bend the rules as needed in reaching people. The issue is not to win at all costs. It is learning to distinguish between what is a timeless standard of behavior, and what is a culturally induced religious tradition. Many of the things we do arise from tradition, not from biblical doctrine in need of preservation.

I have not met Wes Dupin in person, but I relate to him. Wes is building a 21st century Wesleyan ministry in a pretty conservative, Reformed-based part of Michigan. I guess you might say he's reforming the Reformed and unreformed. Daybreak Community Church was planted in 1989 in the Grand Rapids suburb of Hudsonville. It is now one of the largest Wesleyan churches. Known for its innovative ministry to nonchurched seekers, Daybreak has been profiled by Peter Jennings, "In The Name Of God" (ABC documentary). Before starting Daybreak, he directed citywide crusades for fifteen years for his father's ministry. Wes and his wife, Claudia (co-minister at Daybreak), are parents of two sons, Chad and Clint.

"Those who say it cannot be done should get out of the way of those who are doing it." Anonymous

No steeples. No stained glass. No crosses. No robes. No altar rails. No pews. No pulpit. No communion tables. No pipe organs. No choir lofts. No platform with three kingly chairs. No Sunday schools. No Sunday night services. No dreary eighteenth-century hymns. No forced solemnity. No offering plates.

The list has omissions and exceptions, but its implication is clear. Centuries of European tradition and Christian habits are deliberately being abandoned, clearing the way for new forms of worship and congregational culture.

Every church has its own culture—a set of symbols, values and meanings that distinguish it from others. Aside from the more obvious factors such as religious background, polity and social context, each church differs in the messages it sends both to the churched as well as to the unchurched communities. Mood, atmosphere, sight, sound, taste, and smell are all involved. Each congregation has its own "style," its own set of encoded meanings about sacred realities.

We hear many reasons why people drop out of church, quit looking for a church or simply never consider going in the first place. These include the failings of pastors, boring and uninspiring worship services, hypocritical and legalistic people in the pews, lifeless programs, and a generally cold and unfriendly atmosphere. This is a subject about which there is much debate, making many traditional and evangelical church leaders nervous because it implies a rejection of the tried and the once-true and the somehow holy. It also suggests to some an unseemly market-driven approach to building the Kingdom of God.

Recently, our church decided to promote an upcoming Sunday morning message series entitled *"The Adventures of Arnold!"* The subtitles included:

> True Lies - (subject: integrity)
> Predator - (subject: temptation)
> Kindergarten Cop (subject: faith)
> Junior (subject: relationships)
> Eraser (subject: trust)
> Last Action Hero (subject: Jesus is my hero)

The front cover of the two-page folder promoting the series simply read, "I'll Be Back!" Inside it read: Join us for hot music, on-the-edge dramas and stay-awake messages with excellent child care and fun classes for children thru 5th grade! Dress casual and enjoy a drink on the house! (Coffee, of course!) Finally, a church that breaks the mold!" On the back page was a picture of a punk rocker and the message: "All hair styles are welcome!"

The attempt to make our advertising piece for the series relevant to the unchurched provoked this early response on the church's answering machine:

"Hello, this message is for Wes Dupin and anyone else that is interested. I was looking at the Advance Paper (local town newspaper) and I couldn't help but notice your ad in the Advance, and I know you are trying to reach many, many different types of people, but you know I find it interesting that your letter or your notice reads 'Join us for hot music.'

I would like to know since when did Jesus have to advertise hot music and did Jesus ever have to advertise on-the-edge dramas? Did He ever have to advertise . . ." (recording time expired).

(Next Message) Hello, Wes Dupin, I just ran out of time but I also wanted to say in the Bible that I'm reading I don't see where Jesus had to advertise stay-awake messages or excellent child care and fun classes for children. You know, Jesus was a person that people loved to be around. They either loved Him or hated Him, and, uh, I don't know, I don't like this advertising. And also, dress casual and enjoy a drink on the house, I don't believe Jesus had to advertise. Jesus drew people to Him. I hope the best for you. God bless you and I hope you are touched by Him, by Jesus . . . (recording time expired).

(Next Message) "Thank you. I left two prior messages about the advertisement and I just wanted to say one more thing. I find this OOH, kinda slanderous against the body of Christ, Christ Jesus because the last sentence says, finally a church that breaks the mold. Well I would like to know what type of church you are because I belong to the church, the body of Christ and I hope you do too. Bye, Bye."

More recently, it was announced that Elton John would be performing at our city's new arena. The tickets sold out in 41 minutes. How could we relate and reach the Elton John fans? We decided to place an ad on the entertainment page the day of the concert. Here is how it read:

"Dear Elton John:
Welcome to Grand Rapids. Thank you for being a caring friend to Diana. We would like to invite you to our church and if you can't come this Sunday, maybe you can come back for our World Party 2000 on December 31, 1999, at the Van Andel Arena. DAYBREAK . . . 616.669.7733."

Television captured images of the kind of passion and response given to various entertainers and rock groups that had appeared in our community. These images forced me to wrestle with the question, "What are we doing to reach these people?" Talk about stirring up interest and, of course, controversy!

We are supposed to engage in a fierce battle for the lost. We must do whatever it takes to reach these persons, rather than expect them to come to our nice, cozy churches. George Barna puts it this way: "If we hope to include people in the life of the church, we must provide appealing and high quality activities that can successfully compete for people's time, attention and resources. Church programs should include more entertainment related activities." [1]

Martin Luther was a pioneer when it came to reaching the lost with entertaining activities. He often took tunes that were sung in bars and wrote God-inspired words to accompany the melodies. Luther was passionate about reaching the lost. He carefully studied the culture of his day and set out to connect with these people. He believed the three essentials in reaching the lost with the gospel were:

1. Simplicity - keep the message simple so everyone can understand it.
2. Heartfelt relevancy - human drama or an appeal to our emotions and senses is a must.
3. Entertainment - simply a method of reaching the lost.

There is nothing sacred about these principles; they are only attempts to reach lost people with the gospel. Martin Luther wrote: "We ought to direct ourselves in preaching according to the condition of the hearers (heartfelt relevancy) . . . to preach plain and simply (simplicity) is a great art: Christ himself talks of tilling ground, of mustard seed. . . . He used altogether homely and simple similitudes (entertainment)." [2]

For years evangelists like Billy Graham and my father, Clyde Dupin, have used these principles effectively in citywide crusades to reach thousands of lost people with the gospel. Many times their services have been marked by the heartfelt testimony of a professional athlete, a sacred song performed by a Nashville entertainer and a simple gospel message.

I know some church leaders are insulated from the driving force of American entertainment that defines our culture. But it is time for us to get serious about the engagement in the battle for lost souls and minds. We must put forth an aggressive campaign to reach out to these persons instead of expecting them to reach out to us.

I can envision a culturally relevant community of believers who make a positive spiritual difference in our communities. Why shouldn't we be the center of creative arts? Why shouldn't we have a sports center that teaches a healthy, Christ-centered, holistic way of life? Why shouldn't we become the center for creating and developing videos, CDs and movies with positive images and values? This is our moment to seize the opportunity to mobilize our creative spiritual focus and get serious about our culture.

There are no simple formulas, no simple set of criteria that will explain why some churches attract unchurched people and others reject them. The dynamics between a congregation and lost people are complex and unpredictable. Here are some characteristics that unchurched adults are looking for when they go church-shopping, as seen through Daybreak's eyes.

POINT OF RELEVANCE: A church that doesn't whack you on the side of the head.
LESSON: Teach that commitment to church must be freely given.

The church that doesn't "whack you on the side of the head" is a church that respects people and does things in a way that an unchurched person can understand. This church recognizes freedom of choice and relies less on fear. It is a church with some traditions, yet it encourages change. Because our church is located in the center of Dutch culture, many of our people have been raised in a religious system that is very cut and dried. Many have been raised to be in fear—if not petrified—of God. Often the children graduate from their parochial school with resentment toward God and the church. Many times I hear a spiritual struggler say with relief: "I am learning that God loves me just as I am, and He is not really going to 'get me.'"

POINT OF RELEVANCE: Let the walls come down.
LESSON: Invite those who are not members of the church to participate freely with those who are.

I often hear people say, "Daybreak is so friendly and open." Daybreak encourages the breakdown of sexism. Women can deliver the Sunday morning message and serve the elements of communion together with men. We encourage the breakdown of hierarchy. Staff pastors are addressed by first name, not by titles. Tasks such as setting up chairs are shared by lay persons and staff pastors. We encourage the breakdown of Sunday morning fashion shows, reserved parking spots, and the list goes on. We even encourage "sinners or seekers" to play in the band alongside "Christians."

POINT OF RELEVANCE: Be a church where there's a lot of freedom in the basement.
LESSON: Unchurched people need a safe place to explore and investigate Christianity.

Funny thing is, we have no church basement and until recently very few classrooms. What I mean is this, we need to make as many entry points into the mainstream of the church as possible. While there are more formal forms of worship going on upstairs on Sunday mornings, recovery and sharing groups meet in the basement on week nights and weekends. Wade Clark Roof, in *A Generation of Seekers,* refers to this as a sort of ecclesiastical upstairs and downstairs. He writes, "Upstairs is official religion, truth as handed down and defined by authorities; downstairs is religious á la carte, grass-roots spirituality, bricolage, truth as people know it."[3] Develop entry point groups of all kinds (AA, S- Anon, Al-Anon, Alateen, Emotions Anonymous, Overeaters Anonymous, Debtors Anonymous, Divorce and Recovery, Single Again, etc.). Do your best to provide child care and let the newcomers know they are welcome.

POINT OF RELEVANCE: Think like unchurched people.
LESSON: We don't have to agree with our culture, but we must understand it.

I used to direct crusades in various parts of the world for my dad's crusade ministry. Two of the places scheduled were Haiti and Nigeria. Long before my dad and his crusade team would arrive to evangelize the area, it was my responsibility to get a feel for the community, to understand their culture and customs. It is extremely important for us to understand the culture in which we minister. Shortly after arriving in the community in which we planted Daybreak, I visited the Superintendent of Public Schools. I asked him to share with me the social and cultural dynamics of the community. During that very first meeting I found out that teenage pregnancy and alcoholism were growing problems. This gave me a feel for the community and the issues that families faced. My style of teaching, style of worship and the type of church we desired to become were all impacted by these early meetings with community leaders and unchurched people. The more we know about the lifestyles and mind-set of those who live around us, the easier it will be to reach them for Christ.

POINT OF RELEVANCE: Color outside the lines.
LESSON: The worst thing that can happen is nothing.

No one has ever approached me and said, "I absolutely love the changes you are leading us through and here is a million dollars to prove it." If that ever happened, I would probably experience heart failure. Walt Kallestad, pastor of Community Church of Joy, said, "Resistance to change is stronger than any acceptance of the revolutions that are obvious around us." We teach that Jesus Christ is the same yesterday, today and forever, but we present church service styles that are 25, 50 and in some cases a century old.

Church "Super Bowl Parties" have become commonplace today. But when we held our first "Super Bowl Party" in 1991 at the local high school auditorium, not many of the locals had heard of such outlandish ideas, let alone a party on Sunday. However, hundreds showed up with their unchurched friends. Local media, including the ABC and NBC television stations, gave prime-time live reports. The *Grand Rapids Press* made it a front page story.

We communicated that Jesus was interested in parties where sinners hung out and might have even shown up at the Super Bowl, had there been one in Jerusalem. Not everyone was happy with Daybreak's Super Bowl Party. There were protest calls to the high school, letters to the editor, and a school meeting to discuss whether this sort of thing should be allowed.

Listen, resistance to change can be fierce and even warlike. If you are serious about ministering to people the way Jesus did, don't be surprised if some in your community's religious establishment accuse you of selling out to culture and breaking tradition. Remember, it's the trailblazer who gets shot at.

POINT OF RELEVANCE: Rule number one: There are no rules.
LESSON: Employ every imaginable approach so that you might reach
some for Christ.

Jesus only gave this requirement for true worship: "It's who you are and the way you live that count before God. Your worship must engage your spirit in the pursuit of truth. That's the kind of people the Father is out looking for, those who are simply and honestly *themselves* before him in their worship. God is sheer being itself - Spirit. Those who worship him must do it out of their very being, their spirits, their true selves, in adoration" (John 4:23-24 The Message).

God is bored with some of our worship styles. I earnestly believe that He loves change and creativity. There is no prescribed biblical style of worship. One Sunday morning we announced we were having a "Forrest Gump" service. The whole theme of the service centered around outrageous acts of kindness. On entering the church lobby you might have the thought you had stepped into the local movie theater. The atmosphere was that of a movie set and each person was given a bag of popcorn to carry into the main auditorium. Music and drama were reflective of the

"Forrest Gump" film. My message used Forrest and of course his box of "choo-ca-lates" to show in relevant terms the outrageous acts of kindness and love of Jesus Christ. People still refer to that service.

Regardless of stylistic approach, the unchurched need to be impacted with both right brain and left brain.

A major restructuring of religious ecology is underway, particularly in the way the church relates to a growing secular society and culture. I believe we now have the greatest opportunity to present the life-changing gospel to a very savvy culture. We need not mess with the message, but rather with the medium of how it is expressed. Take the risk and use the most innovative medium possible to effectively communicate the love of Jesus Christ.

Relevancy Bytes Memory Acronym

R Risk changes that will reach unchurched people.

E Encourage creative and innovative ways of doing church.

L Love unchurched people without boundaries.

E Enlist the help of community leaders to understand local culture.

V Value the comments of unchurched people.

A Attend concerts, movies and art events that attract the people you are trying to reach.

N Never give up on reaching the lost.

C Carefully develop your strategy in reaching unchurched people.

Y Your mission is changed lives—nothing more, nothing less.

B Be a risk taker.

Y Your focus should be on opportunities, not on problems.

T Trust God always.

E Expect God's best.

S Serve God with joy.

ENDNOTES

[1]George Barna, *The Frog in the Kettle* (Venture, Cal.: Regal Books, 1992), p. 93.

[2]Thomas S. Kepler, ed., *The Table Talk of Martin Luther* (New York: World, 1952), quoted in Walt Kallested, *Entertainment Evangelism* (Nashville: Abingdon, 1996), p. 10.

[3]Wade Clark Roof, *A Generation of Seekers* (New York: Harper Collins, 1993), p. 210.

Chapter 6

Church Health

by Marty Grubbs

*T*rees which cease to grow, cease to live. Like most living things, growth is a sign of health. Exceptions exist, but generally a lack of growth reveals a lack of health. We fool ourselves by thinking we can have significant quality growth without quantity growth as a side effect. If this is true, well over 85% of American congregations lack sufficient health to stimulate growth.

While most of the church growth talk these days has to do with cultural relevance—meaning seeker sensitivity, the use of multimedia and drama, and new paradigm principles—an underlying principle persists: church health. Just as there are numerous unhealthy traditional congregations, there are also many unhealthy new paradigm congregations. Those of us in the new paradigm culture sometimes overestimate the cutting-edge concepts and underestimate basic congregational health. Having said that, the tendency is to overestimate the well-being of our own congregation. We hope for the best and like to think things are just fine.

Sometimes we look at growing churches and assume that we'd be healthy too, if we had growth. The sequence is that growth is a by-product of health. Most of us prefer hanging around healthy people, physically and emotionally, versus unhealthy ones. The same is true of churches. There is a fresh, invigorating sense of contagion when you are around healthy congregations. You can almost feel it in the parking lot and foyer. The energy embraces you as you enter the sanctuary. People *are often at a loss for words when cornered for a response to their attendance. Is it the message? The music? The youth or children's program? Maybe. But the intangible bottom line is vitality. The result is that healthy congregations grow.*

Marty Grubbs understands congregational health. He pastors a vibrant church in Oklahoma City called Belle Isle Community Church (Church of God Anderson). Belle Isle has effectively ministered to its community, which is in the higher rent district. In the twelve years of his pastorate, the church has grown from under 150 to over 1700 in average worship attendance. Belle Isle's blended worship style is not unique to many holiness churches, but a sense of health permeates its programs, engaging people to grow their souls.

Church Health

It was late September of 1985 and I was facing what seemed to be the decision of my life. The search committee had requested that I attend their meeting that Monday night. I assumed they would want me to suggest individuals for the position of new senior pastor. Since I had grown up in the church and was a third-generation church staff member, they surely thought I would know some people they ought to contact. The evening took a turn I did not anticipate. They looked at me and asked, "Would you be our next senior pastor?"

I will admit to having given it some thought after our former pastor resigned and moved to the west coast. In my most serious moments, I concluded it was not a good idea. Besides, I had just accepted a position with a wonderful church and was about to announce to the search committee that the new senior pastor would have the privilege of choosing his own associate.

It wasn't that I was so much opposed to the role of senior pastor as it was that I had prepared myself more for associate ministry. I yearned for the behind-the-scenes work of a church. Growing up in a pastor's home, I knew how vital that work was. I felt confident of my administrative gifts. I was close to completing my degree in business administration after completing majors in religious studies and sacred music. I had visions of pursuing an MBA. My lifelong dream was the sacred music business. The kindness of a long friendship with Bill and

Gloria Gaither had created my appetite for the industry. Nonetheless, I had accepted the call to be the associate pastor of this small church of 150 people in Oklahoma City. Now, four years later, they wanted me to be their pastor.

My honest evaluation of their request was not very positive. I saw several obstacles. I had not attended seminary and I had no formal theological training outside an undergraduate degree in religious studies. Could the associate pastor be an effective senior pastor in the same church? I had seen few instances where this had worked. My wife had been a part of this church from birth. Could they let her grow up and be their pastor's wife? To this I added my own sense that this church needed an older and more experienced senior pastor. Their first two pastors had each stayed ten years. The last two young pastors had each stayed two years. I just knew they needed a wise man with an impressive track record who would commit to stay for at least five years.

Less than eight weeks later, I was the new senior pastor of the Westridge Hills Church of God (Anderson) in northwest Oklahoma City. We averaged 143 in church that month. Twelve and a half years later we were just shy of 1700 in average weekly attendance. Occasionally I find myself sitting at my desk (in what used to be our foyer) and asking, "What happened? How did we get here?"

While I remember several key decisions along the way, it is much easier to look back and see the critical factors that created the atmosphere for growth in our church. Following are a few things we did with great courage and purpose in those early years. I conclude with ten key factors that God has seemed to use to bring us where we are today.

During my first two years, we began to see numerical growth. Our average Sunday morning had grown from 143 to almost 180. This was not significant growth to anyone else, but to the dear people who had helped plant this church in 1959, it was very significant. At 180, our small sanctuary was beginning to feel cramped. I remember the day that the chairman of the Board of Trustees, Tom Webb, came to me and suggested we pull out the old master plan and give thought to the construction of a larger sanctuary. I was somewhat enthused, yet the memories of growing up in several building fund campaigns also created a bit of fear in me.

Tom's suggestion turned out to be a significant step in the process of growth for our church. We built a 500-seat sanctuary and did two other important things at the same time. First, we cleaned up the rest of the building, bringing the facility out of the sixties and into the eighties. Secondly, we changed the name of the church. "Westridge Hills" was not identifiable to anyone. The community had been originally platted to be known as Westridge Hills, but the prominence of nearby Belle Isle Lake had actually created the identity for the area. Everyone knew the area as "Belle Isle." We became Belle Isle. The next part of the name, Church of God, seemed to be a continual barrier and was an identity problem. People assumed us to be very different than what we actually were. Some visited and left, disappointed that we were not the Church of God they were seeking. Many more stayed away out of fear that we were the Church of God of which they had heard. We felt the word community would better communicate our mission. In April of 1988, the letters attached to the front of the new sanctuary read, "Belle Isle Community Church." It was no small accomplishment that the facility and name changes were done by the church in complete unity, harmony and with not one penny of debt.

Other significant decisions we could not have predicted impacted our church. A lay leader came to me and suggested that we do a major advertising campaign. With a new sanctuary and name, we needed to immediately convey our new identity to the community. He gave the money to accomplish this goal. We asked a local graphic artist to design door hangers that would inform the community about us and provide them with a schedule of activities. We placed 3000 of these on doors in our neighborhood.

We put ads in newspapers and on the radio. I gave a sermon series based on the themes most often recognized in the 12-Step ministry of Alcoholics Anonymous. I used twelve themes from the scriptures and pointed out that the God of our own understanding could only be understood through Jesus Christ. The reception in the community was tremendous. The visitor flow was significant. Despite being located in one of the most affluent areas of Oklahoma City, there was tremendous interest in these twelve themes.

Another significant decision that paved the way for continued growth was the addition of a small-group ministry in place of the traditional Sunday night service. It would never have worked if we had simply one day announced that we would no longer have a Sunday evening service. I put together a two-year plan and initiated it by contacting ten families in our church, asking them to open their homes for a dessert fellowship after our Sunday night service. By the time we were meeting every Sunday night, the congregation was wondering what took us so long. We now break up the year into three primary semesters, with breaks during holidays and a few weeks during summer.

Another important step that has brought big dividends was inviting key lay leaders to attend some church growth conferences with me. I began to take lay persons with me to any conference I attended. I found that when key leaders and people with a passion for the church attended conferences with me, we came home with a new determination. I did not have to return alone and try to convince everyone to do something I had learned we should do. This trend continues today. I cannot begin to calculate the results of a motivated laity.

Another key move was to make a commitment to stay ahead of the growth instead of reacting to it. This meant consistent training on my part along with other lay leaders. As we approached four hundred in attendance, we attended one of John Maxwell's "Beyond 800" conferences. If we were to grow to that level, we needed to know what it would look and feel like and how it might affect us. We hired staff in anticipation of growth. We had three full-time pastoral staff members in place before we hit 400. By the time we hit 500 in worship, there were six full-time pastoral staff members, one full-time administrative director and three secretaries. In addition to my role as senior pastor, we had a full-time minister of music, two full-time youth ministers, a full-time children's minister, and a full-time minister of Christian education.

These are just a few of the steps we took with our eyes open and hearts full of faith. They were intentional steps to be the church we felt God had called us to be in this community. Everything was done because these people had a passion for the things of God, a passion for excellence and a desire to be a clear expression of the Biblical community God had in mind from the beginning.

Our church also grew when very wounded people from other churches showed up on our doorstep. In the early 90s an unfortunate number of high profile churches in Oklahoma City ran into great difficulty. Among the problems were financial disasters resulting from millions of dollars of debt that could not be paid when the oil boom "went bust." Several local pastors also suffered through moral, ethical and financial problems. God seemed to be using Belle Isle as a place of healing for many who were ready to give up on the church. The quest for numerical growth must never focus on reaching people in other churches, but we were enjoying church health at a time when many wounded and godly people were disillusioned and confused.

When I am asked to speak to other church leaders about church growth, I first tell them that church growth must not be the goal; rather, the focus must be church health. When a church is healthy, it can grow—not just numerically, but spiritually. We were a healthy church. The Bible uses the word "body" to exemplify the church. A body is healthy when it is in good shape, meaning you can take the steps when the elevator isn't working. Good shape means you can exert energy at a moment's notice, that all the major systems in the human body are functioning at optimal levels. The church is healthy when it is committed to God's Word and not comfortable traditions. Traditions are not wrong or evil, but far too many Christians get upset about a deviation from traditions, while not shedding a tear in a church that was unfriendly to a nonbeliever. I often find that we are more committed to the hymnal than we are the Bible. The church must be firmly rooted in God's Word and this must be accomplished from the pulpit as well as in the classroom.

A church is healthy when there is a clear understanding of one another's gifts and abilities. A church is healthy when the pastor does not feel the need to be the center of authority. More pastors need to be asking themselves, "How can I serve these people?" instead of asking, "How can I get these people to follow me?" When egos and power get in the way, they cause great difficulty. A church is healthy when it lives within its means. To always be asking the church people to bail out a busted budget can be very defeating to the members and certainly repulsive to a visiting unbeliever. It can also raise questions of trust concerning the elected leaders. A church is healthy when it is willing to take steps of faith. Approving an aggressive budget is all right, so long as you commit to living within the income.

The church is healthy when there is unity. I am a consensus builder. I have made few decisions alone. One of the only decisions I consistently make on my own is what to preach on Sunday. I have found great success in pulling teams of people together to research and discuss a possible change in the church program, the potential addition of a new staff member, a name change or the feasibility of a new building.

If I had announced to our people some of the big changes we have made without first involving them, most of the changes would have never taken place. Thankfully, my ego needs were small and the people appreciated being considered and consulted in the various processes. When I speak of consensus building, I do not automatically mean the formation of committees. I have seen committees used as a tool to involve people. There is nothing wrong with this as long as the committee has a clear reason to meet and can make decisions that are then carried out. Our church constitution says very little about committees. We have the freedom to form ministry teams as needed and let them off the hook when the task is accomplished.

These things have contributed to what I feel is a very healthy church. Because it is in good health, it continues to grow. We will soon move into our new 200,000 square foot facility on 77 acres, complete with facilities for each ministry area and a 3500 seat sanctuary. It has been a journey of faith. We have stretched and trusted God and stood in amazement as we have seen Him lead and provide. This eighteen million dollar facility is paid for. We will not have a large monthly interest payment to make. Instead, we will hire staff and expand our mission work in the city and beyond.

As I look back on the past 13 years, I see ten key ingredients that created a healthy church in northwest Oklahoma City. These factors helped us get where we are and they will help us continue in our growth.

1. Discernment

Paul prayed that we might be able to "discern what is best" in Philippians 1:10.

David asked God for discernment because he was God's servant (Ps. 119:125). The senior pastor must pray for discernment in two areas. The first is his/her personal life. In *The 21st Century Pastor*, David Fisher says we must ask the question, "Who am I?"[1] What are my strengths, weaknesses, temptations, gifts and talents? I must have the courage to face these truths. I will not be an effective leader, especially in a growing church, if I do not have a grasp of who I am. It is clear to me that I possess certain gifts which God uses to get His work done at Belle Isle. I also know that I have some areas of weakness and must surround myself with leadership and staff who have strengths in these areas.

A second area in which we must pray for discernment is the people. Who are they? What are they like? If I should ever pastor another congregation, I would first ask these questions before I would try anything that worked in the previous church. A management expert said, "One of the greatest tasks of leadership is to define reality, to see things as they really are." To do this takes a great deal of time to get to know your people and your community. It is very important that the church have a clear understanding of what is happening in the community because this shapes the culture of the church.

When the Murrah Federal Building in downtown Oklahoma City was bombed in April 1996, we were all in a state of shock and panic. In the months that followed, it became clear that our community had changed. To have missed that observation or to assume that we could go back to business as usual, was to have missed a wonderful moment for ministry in this community. We must commit to defining reality in our lives and in the lives of our people.

2. Trust

When a pastor is willing to be a student of his own life and people, he will make decisions that will serve the people of the church. The decision will be implemented in appropriate ways. When this happens, the people begin to trust you. When you are trusted as a pastor, your people will be more forgiving when you disappoint them or cause them discomfort in implementing change. Trust is built when people know two things:

a) That you love them and have as your major focus a desire to serve and lead them in a closer walk with God.
b) When your own spiritual journey is vibrant, real and transparent.

People have difficulty following a pastor who is arrogant or who tries to appear as perfect. When people know that you have a thorn or two, they will trust you.

Most of what has taken place at Belle Isle would not have happened if I had not been building trust with my people. In my eighth year as their pastor, it was trust that helped them take a major leap of faith in building a 200,000 square foot facility. They trusted my judgment and my commitment to them. This was certainly not the only driving factor in this decision, but I know my people and they would not have taken this step with a pastor they did not trust.

3. Unity

Discernment enabled me to build trust with my people. This created a tremendous sense of unity. A key role for the senior pastor in maintaining unity is conflict resolution. We must discern when there is potential conflict and help people solve issues before they become ignited by emotions. The role of a good shepherd is to see trouble coming and deal with it, even before the sheep realize it is on the horizon. When this is done, the unity of the church is protected.

Communication is another key role in maintaining unity. Never assume your people understand all the details. They don't. The larger the church gets, the more critical it is to communicate consistently and clearly. You cannot assume that just because you said it once that it need not be repeated.

Consensus building has been another key in our unity. We have pulled together teams of people in every area of ministry. I have required that staff members have an advisory council that meets monthly to provide input and direction. The staff members are to be chairpersons of the councils. They have total freedom in deciding who will be on the council. I ask for a final look at the names of the persons they will include, just in case there are problems or conflicts of which they may not be aware. The persons on these ministry teams are people involved in the ministry area, giving time and resources, and displaying a cooperative and serving attitude. This has played a vital role in maintaining our unity.

4. Leadership

When you have discernment that leads to trust and unity, you then have won the right to lead your people. I am now able to take far more initiative in decision making than I did ten years ago. There are some areas where I must lead without a consensus group behind me. Leadership means I am willing to make the tough calls. Leadership means I take responsibility instead of looking for someone to blame. Leadership means I let my people win. Leadership does the right thing for the good of the church, whether or not your people recognize it or applaud you for it. Leadership initiates. Leadership waits for the right time.

A good leader recognizes the magnitude of the responsibility. Good leaders know what may be permissible yet not beneficial (1 Cor. 6:12). Leadership breaks down future plans and decisions into bite-size pieces and allows time for people to embrace them. Leadership does not necessarily mean that you are out in front of your people, carrying a torch and yelling, "Charge!"

5. Vision

I used to cringe when I'd hear a leader at a church growth conference telling us we needed to cast a vision. I squirmed hearing again that where there is no vision people perish. I had a tough time getting this one down. What is vision? A vision is a clear mental picture of a preferred future. It has been increasingly important for me to keep a vision of the future before our people. Where are we going? What do we want to look like in five years, ten years, fifteen years? Bobb Biehl has been especially helpful to me in this area. Bobb has an unusual gift for asking questions. It has been through his questions that we have formulated a vision for the church. Willow Creek Community Church has been another source of inspiration in this area. They use the term "unique thumbprint" to describe their church. It has been a very helpful exercise to determine what our church's unique thumbprint is in this community.

Vision must be constantly communicated. I find that I can make vision statements in almost any sermon. I can see in many texts the result or teaching concerning the kind of church we are and want to continue to be. When you are trusted and when there is unity, people are not afraid of vision. People of faith require a vision to keep them challenged and focused.

6. Clarity of Mission

Bobb Biehl asks two questions concerning our congregation;

a) What will you always do?
b) What will you never do?

These wonderful questions have enabled the leadership of our church to have clarity concerning the direction of the church. These questions help us accept the fact that there are many things we will not or cannot do. They help us establish a sense of peace about ourselves and who we are.

For instance, we would never open a soup kitchen in our church. It is not because we don't want to. It is not because we are not missions-minded. Our church is nowhere near the place a soup kitchen is needed. By partnering with churches in areas of town where there are needs for soup kitchens, we can do a much better job than if we had one at our church.

Another example is that we use a blend of musical styles in our worship. One worship service will start with a classical brass quintet and move to a praise band and contemporary choruses. We sing "O God, Our Help In Ages Past" and "In The Lord Alone" in the same service. We use a full orchestra with a one-hundred-voice choir. We are able to do completely traditional and more formal styles of worship, and we can do an entirely contemporary service. But we know that God has called us to provide a careful blend of both. We follow the exact worship format in all three of our services and we believe that this is very important.

There must be clarity in the mission of the church, embraced by staff and leadership and communicated constantly. When someone comes to our church and wants us to begin a door-to-door visitation ministry, we can point to our commitment to call first before visiting someone's home. When that person disagrees and leaves our church, we are not disappointed. We are clear about how we are going to do assimilation and follow-up. Surveys of new people attending our church consistently tell us that our lack of contact after their first visit was the deciding factor in their visiting our church a second time.

Knowing what you will and will never do is freeing.

7. Finances

Churches can become divided into the haves and the have nots. One of the primary areas of our growth comes from our local community. We happen to be a few blocks from some of the most expensive real estate in the state of Oklahoma. People sitting behind the gates of an estate have the same spiritual needs as those sitting in a small apartment. Money can make people look better, but it never makes us feel better. We have reached many people who were as down-and-out as anybody I have seen, but they had tremendous earning power or resources. They now have a personal relationship with Jesus, maturing in a church that did not treat them differently because of their address or assets.

We must keep several things in mind where this subject is concerned. We must not treat people differently, elevate those with money to positions of leadership, or name buildings after those who give in significant ways to the church. This is not biblical and usually creates more trouble than it is worth.

We must clearly teach biblical stewardship. I have had to apologize to my congregation for not teaching it. Because the subject of money can be a stumbling block to a nonbeliever or a visitor to the church, I would not mention it from the pulpit for years. I realized that I was denying my people the wonderful teaching of God's blessings and the joy of seeing God at work in their lives. I now preach a three or four week series on stewardship each year. We also consistently teach these concepts in our newcomers classes, Bible studies, and discipleship ministry. We find that it is received much better once we have established a relationship and our motives are trusted. We ask people to give based on the biblical teachings. We do not ask them to give because we cannot pay a bill or because we are in debt. We have never had any debt and we have not approached the congregation due to difficulty in paying any bill. This would signal problems in the church.

Another key factor in our ability to raise money has been the strong economy we are enjoying in the late 90s. After careful research, we suggested several ways a person could give to our church, blessing the church and letting the person receive tremendous tax benefits. Never underestimate the value of educating yourself in ways for people to give. We received two gifts of stock for the construction of our new facility. The donors received tax benefits from the donation and—surprise—the value of the stock doubled several times. The gifts were responsible for 50% of the cost of our new facility!

God will use our resources to get His work done. It is a tough job, but we must teach our people the joy of giving.

8. Staff

Staff will make or break a church. I credit our staff for the wonderful church we have become. Because of our commitment to stay out of debt, we have been able to hire staff and build ministries instead of making interest payments.

Hire as soon as you can. Always be on the lookout for someone you believe would be able to lead the ministry assignment to health and growth. Hire the best you can. I have hired staff that are older, better educated, and as a result, better paid than me. I remember the time I had to convince our board to hire a staff member and pay him significantly more than I was making as senior pastor. This was one of the best decisions we ever made in the staffing area. Never settle for second best. Hire the best person you can find to lead the ministry you are staffing.

Hire staff using clearly defined job descriptions. All staff should know what is expected of them, who they are to report to, and how they will be evaluated. Yearly raises should keep pace with inflation and when possible, rewards should be given for their efforts. If they are not working hard or being effective, tell them so, and do not give raises when they are not deserved.

These issues are best handled by a Personnel Committee, not the entire board (or council) and certainly not by the congregation at large.

9. Facilities

Facilities must never be the main objective of the church, but should accomplish two things:

a) Facilities must be functional. Do not let a building hinder what God wants to do in the life of the church. We have moved many walls as we have grown, which resulted in better working environments, more room for growth, and happier staff or lay volunteers.

b) Facilities must match who you are. Your work and worship space say a lot about who you are and what you do. They are your greatest advertisement. Make sure your facility matches the surrounding neighborhood properties. Keep your neighbors pleased with your presence in their community. A church that is an eyesore or lowers surrounding property values is a poor testimony.

These are the days of multiple purpose needs in facilities. I admire churches that have built attractive houses of worship that can also serve as a fellowship hall or gymnasium. Your ministry is greatly enhanced by having these options.

10. The Future

A final ingredient in building healthy, growing churches is to always prepare for the future. We need not focus on the future at the expense of the present, but a good leader will always keep an eye on the horizon.

In *Built To Last*, James Collins wrote that the clear need for the leader of any organization is to prepare the organization for health without him or her.[2] I have to ask myself occasionally, "What can I do to help this church remain healthy, even when I am no longer the pastor?"

Many times when a pastor leaves, he makes an announcement to the congregation and four weeks later he is gone. I think one of the greatest gifts an outgoing pastor can give his congregation is to assist them in the process of finding his replacement. I do not mean he should serve on the search committee. He should not have a vote or a final say. But a departing pastor can tremendously help the church he leaves by providing direction or potential candidates for the church to consider.

We must keep a watchful eye on the future. What ministry is growing in such a way that a full-time staff member may be needed to keep it healthy? What additions to the facility could meet the needs of a growing concern in your church or community? Keeping an eye on the future enables the church to effectively and relevantly minister in the present.

ENDNOTES

[1]David Fisher, *The 21st Century Pastor: A Vision Based on the Ministry of Paul,* (Grand Rapids: Zondervan Publishing House, 1996), p. 37.
[2]James C. Collins, Jerry I. Porres (contributor), *Built to Last: Successful Habits of Visionary Companies* (San Francisco: HarperBusiness, 1997), p. 158.

Chapter 7

Future Church Worship and the Arts

21st Century Worship *by Mark Cork*

Using Technology to Enhance Worship *by Jonathan Foster*

Drama and Arts Come to Church *by Nancy Nelson*

*O*ne of the most controversial subjects in the church today is the
style of worship. What used to divide congregations—tongues,
eternal security, doctrinal issues, etc.—have been replaced by
worship style preferences, namely music and the arts. This
tension has much more to do with cultural differences than
theology. Sociologists know that music is one of the most important

purveyors of cultural characteristics. Our disagreements are not logical; they are emotional. That helps us understand why educated, civil people can become so argumentative over such things as hymns vs. praise choruses, pipe organs vs. drums, not to mention dance and multimedia. We tend to sanctify our cultural preferences and strive feverishly to support our bias biblically . . . to no avail. The Bible does not give us narrowly defined worship styles. You'll never read about pipe organs or Martin Luther's, Fanny Crosby's, or Charles Wesley's songs in the New Testament. Most of the traditions we perceive as ageless were new a few centuries or even decades ago.

New paradigm churches are not antitraditional. They don't preach against pipe organs, hymnals, or liturgy. Rather, new paradigm ministry is about helping people experience culturally relevant, genuine worship, which means different things to different people. This chapter is not about the perennial tension regarding worship styles in so many congregations. It is about learning how to understand what sort of worship style characterizes a majority of the growing, thriving churches across America. The arts are coming back to church. If we are to reach generations which have been raised on multimedia, we must become more entertaining and stimulating in church. The word entertain literally means "to hold in tension." It should not be perceived as evil or secular to hold people's attention. Jesus used it in His day, only then it took the form of story telling. Creating engaging tension in our services helps people listen and actively participate in worship. To bore people with the gospel is a sin. You can't convert or disciple sleeping pew occupants.

Mark Cork is a cutting-edge worship leader whose desire is to help the unchurched find God via engaging worship and communication styles. Mark has served in a contemporary church plant, coordinated several denominational events, and offers resources to churches seeking contemporary and blended worship formats. He is the worship pastor at First Church of the Nazarene in Houston, Texas, and is married to Jackie. Mark helps us understand the big picture in reaching people in today's culture, without advocating a specific style.

Jonathan Foster is the worship pastor at Scottsdale Family Church. As a song writer and leading-edge worship leader, he gives us a look at the role of technology in using audiovisual equipment to reach the media-drenched people in our society. Jonathan is married to Johnna and is dad to Quincy and Shay.

Nancy Nelson is an ordained women's minister on staff at Scottsdale Family Church and formerly at Skyline Wesleyan. Her role in writing, directing, and acting in drama gives us insights on how the dramatic arts can help communicate the Good News in ways which engage people. Nancy is married to Alan and is mom to Jeffrey, Joshua, and Jesse.

21st Century Worship

Knowing How to Plan

The typical church spends the bulk of its ministry doing good things like caring for the sick, teaching the Bible, providing age appropriate programs and opportunities for socializing. For the most part, churches care for their own quite adequately. But how about the people who don't attend? How well does the typical church do at reaching those in the community who call no church home? How is the church designing its public services to attract these people? How is this growing segment of our population going to be reached if we don't passionately, intentionally pursue them?

These questions are becoming increasingly important. The way a church answers them is a true indicator of how serious it is in pursuing the Great Commission. Will we continue business as usual? Or will we begin seeing the lost and care about them enough to redesign the way we "do church" to attract them? The future of our churches is not in emphasizing ministries and services predominantly for the churched, because these numbers are dwindling in a post-modern society. The key is in reaching the unchurched, predominantly through inspiring, user-friendly worship services which return people to God.

Today's consumers are beginning to protest the one-size-fits-all approach that was so popular not long ago. They want to make sure they are specifically cared for, so they often feel more comfortable when part of a niche. This desire means they will probably be with people who share their ideals and tastes, allowing relationships to develop more quickly and last longer. Knowing it can't be all things to all people, today's smart church defines who it is and who it isn't. It knows which niche or niches it wants to reach and then develops services to appeal to its market. When programming the public service(s), knowing your niche is a necessity.

I was recently involved in a project with Hallmark, the greeting card company, which involved discussing a new store concept with one of the corporation's directors. In creating this new store, Hallmark wanted to design a place that would attract non-Hallmark customers. Consumer research told executives what this new store should look like because they asked non-Hallmark customers what kind of store would attract them. They asked, "What do we need to do to get you to shop at a Hallmark store?"

How could we apply these principles to the church? What if we designed a church based on the input of people who don't attend church? What would it look like? What would it sound like? When would it be open? What services would it offer? What would the public service look like? Lyle Schaller once told me, "We need to design our services for the people not yet coming." The Hallmark concept certainly fits the Schaller approach. But how do we gather such vital information without hiring a large market research firm?

One natural answer is to rely on the research of successful churches which have won our respect, like Willow Creek Community Church. One problem with their research, however, is that it was originally done about 20 years ago. A lot has changed since then. Another is that the research was done for a specific location. What works in a Midwest metropolitan area may or may not work in another area of the country.

Instead of relying on others, develop your own creative ways to get information on the people you are targeting. Gather a small group of people from your church community who match your target. Ask them which radio stations they and their friends listen to most. Then contact the advertising or marketing departments of those radio stations and ask them for a breakdown of their listeners' demographics. This is a common practice with people in advertising, and the information is readily available and usually free. What they provide can tell you the listeners' basic likes and dislikes, what they do with their spare time and money, their ages, their income, a family profile, hobbies and other information that will help you program a service attractive to them. Listen to those stations to see what musical styles your target group enjoys.

Another option is to gather similar people within your church to help create a focus group. The goal is to get groups of unchurched people together for the purpose of finding out what kind of church would be attractive to them. In other words, "What kind of church would we need to create to get you to attend?" When you have willing participants, ask them to host informal receptions in their homes. They should invite a few of their close, unchurched friends to come for dessert and discussion. Stress that the host should be up-front with guests about the purpose of the meeting, but make the point that this is not a pressure tactic to get people to come to church. It is only a focus group, intended to gather information helpful to the church. During this reception, hosts could ask guests why they don't go to church, whether they've ever gone to church regularly, and the kind of church that would be appealing to them.

Once the focus groups have met and compiled their notes, you should have a clearer understanding of the church type your target group would find appealing. Maybe they want a service on Sunday night only or not on Sunday at all. Maybe they want a church where they can wear jeans, sit around tables and drink coffee during the service. Maybe they want a church that offers after-school programs one night a week, where their kids can get help with homework, and then be joined by their parents for dinner and worship. The important thing is that you find the needs for your area and respond. You might discover they don't want a lot of what you're offering. If that's the case, quit offering it and give them what they want! You need not compromise on the message to change the methodology.

Knowing What to Plan

Now that we have some perspective on the type of church your target people want, it's time to consider how to build the service they'll find appealing. When beginning this process it's vital to remember three things:

1. Your target profile.
2. Each person is at a different point in understanding the gospel.
3. Each person is entering with a different heritage and perspective (with different biases, expectations, etc.).

Our job as church leaders is to unify those differences, so that everyone arrives at the intended goal for that service. Therefore, first define the starting point of the service and how it will affect the participant.

The starting point is when people first walk into your auditorium. What is the atmosphere like? Are you beginning to tell them something about the service by what they see and hear? Does the visual climate begin taking them toward the intended goal for that particular service or does it look and sound the same every week?

Creating an atmosphere may be as simple as projecting your service theme on a screen or altering the style of music each week so that stylistically it begins to set the stage for the service. It could be more complicated or ambitious, like playing back-to-back movie clips that support the theme of the service. For example, if you're beginning a series on time management, you could project a countdown clock showing the number of minutes until the service starts or have the printed program list the number of minutes each service element is expected to last. If the theme is on stress, the pre-service music could alternate stressful and soothing styles. If an element of the message uses a small prop like a rubber band or paper clip to illustrate a point, consider handing one to each person as they arrive. Their curiosity will be piqued and their minds energized. Whatever the approach, do it with quality and intentionality.

Once you've created an engaging atmosphere, plan how to engage multiple senses during the service. People no longer want just a service; they seek an experience. They are looking for something that is more hands-on than the typical spectator approach to church we've offered for so long. It is becoming increasingly important to stimulate multiple senses when you communicate. When I was a child, it was common to hear a TV announcer tell you about an upcoming program while you saw the closing credits of a show. Now the standard is to see credits, hear a voice-over, and see visuals of a new show. ESPN gives multiple levels of information throughout each broadcast. Almost continually, you can see sports scores or information about other events scrolling across the bottom of your screen while you watch the main broadcast. FOX News anchors report a story while supportive graphics simultaneously tell you about other aspects of that story. Communication which engages multiple senses is becoming the norm. We run the risk of losing our audience if we don't at least offer some type of multiple stimuli. Here are a few possibilities:

- Song lyrics projected over static background.
- Song lyrics projected over slow-moving video background.
- Video clips to support service theme.
- Video clips "within" a live drama.
- Video testimonies woven between live testimonies.
- Scripture reading from someone in the audience with words on-screen.
- Message supported by Power Point or other computer presentation program, plus take-home handouts.
- Message supported by video clips or "on-the-street" video interviews with pre-Christians.
- Invite volunteers on stage to participate in a visual illustration (if

- Scenic video on screen behind a vocal soloist.
- Children's choir singing in service via "live broadcast" from another part of the building (no more watching the kids march in and waiting for them to get into place before they can sing—great time saver).

At the end of the service, after you've given them all you've got, what's the desired response? What do they do with what you've given them? How do they live in response to what they've seen, heard and experienced? Just as you carefully plan the other components, the end must also be strategically planned and executed. Why go to all the work of making the other components strong and then throw it out the window with a weak ending? Should the people make a verbal response? What is happening musically to reinforce the theme? Should there be a final visual image for people to grasp that will come back to them during the week? Should they take home a reminder of the service like a bookmark or a refrigerator magnet that will challenge them to live out the experience they've just had?

What are you doing to get them back next week? What are the hooks or tie-ins for next week? How about an announcer giving highlights of next week's service while the band plays? If you have a special children's event scheduled, have a child come in and promote it rather than just hand out a promotional flyer. Do you have a refreshment time after the service where you can reinforce the experience of the service or promote next week's service? Whatever you do, don't let "amen" be the last word!

Bringing people to the Lord has always been a creative enterprise. What happened in Mark, chapter two, when the men bringing the paralytic to Jesus couldn't get to Him because of the crowds? They got creative! They cut a hole in the roof and lowered their friend to Jesus. This couldn't have been an easy process, or an easy thing to explain to the homeowner, but it was the only way they could get their friend to Jesus.
Risky? Yes!
Daring? Without a doubt!
Original? Of course!
Worth it? You bet!

When it comes to bringing people to Jesus, there are no right or wrong methods—only effective or ineffective. Our task is to find those that are effective and practice them with a fiery passion.

Using Technology to Enhance Worship

Our society's piqued interest in the spiritual realm coupled with our zest for the arts makes it a fantastic time for Christian artists and communicators. With a little creativity and some divine inspiration, being culturally relevant in the 21st century should be the rule and not the exception. Churches can now create memorable graphics and eye-catching videos at a fraction of the time and cost it took even five years ago. The variety of music available for the local church is mind-boggling. The line between professional and amateur drama sketches, visual aids and dance continues to blur every day.

Churches often get a bad rap when it comes to their unwillingness to implement technology. Frequently it's deserved, but sometimes the issue is simply finances. Have you ever seen dollar signs in board members' eyes when you brought up a new idea? Do you hear the finance committee mumble "cha-ching" when you walk by? If you have, then join the thousands of us who proudly wear the title of music pastor, worship leader, program director, etc. To put it mildly, it's difficult to be on the cutting-edge when the funding is dull. What we lack in finances we often have to make up in creativity.

- Recently, we secured some excellent rates at a local editing suite and produced 500, seven minute videotapes to hand to potential attendees. Total cost for us was $800, plus 12-15 hours of time.
- We wanted to showcase the children one morning, so we fitted a regular video camera with an extra long cable, went to children's church and projected the children live on our screen during the offertory. Total cost was the price of a long cable and an hour putting it together.
- Our internet page was created and is maintained by volunteers. Cost to the church was a few hours of consultation.
- Some musicians from the community donate time to the church because some of our players do the same for them in other venues. Cost: a few hours.
- The internet allows us to network and obtain ideas with greater efficiency every day for sermon illustrations, publicity, resources and technological breakthroughs.

The use of volunteers is critical, but this is no excuse for poor performance. If we are going to try something new, it's important we do it well. Nothing kills a great idea faster than weak execution. Worship and arts pastor, Monty Kelso said, "We stand out from the norm by consistently delivering a high quality of creative expression and communication." Pre-Christians are inundated with a high quality of creative communication from secular media. If we intend to captivate them, we should be prepared to deliver comparable quality.

Many of us deal with people who are concerned about tradition. In the proper perspective, tradition can guide us in our attempt to be culturally relevant. Jazz bassist Lislie Ellis says, "Jazz is an arrow. The shaft is time. The feathers are history/tradition keeping it on course. The tip is the avant-garde group that penetrates the resistance to change."[1] Church work is similar, *although sometimes we feel like we're splattering rather than penetrating.* The avant-garde group consists of churches and people who are looking for new ways to reach others for Christ. They're connected to the rest of the arrow, but they're out front . . . penetrating. For the gospel to spread in North America, we need penetrators: people who are changing, seeking and asking. Jesus encourages us by saying that whoever seeks will find, whoever asks will receive and whoever knocks on the door will have the door opened (Matt. 7:7). Seeking, asking, knocking; that's how we find our unique calling. The writer of Proverbs, chapter two, exhorts us to search for wisdom as we would for a hidden treasure. Anyone who has ever searched for treasure will attest to the excitement that accompanies the search. We can be equally excited about the kind of vision God is going to give us. Every congregation doesn't need to be a giant church. We need more everyday, ordinary churches finding their life-long, extraordinary call. We don't need imitators; we need initiators. Every individual has unique gifts and visions, as well as every church. If this is true then it also makes sense to say that every communication and arts department within a given church will have unique gifts and visions. To be culturally relevant, it's not enough to be like somebody else. We should find out what the Holy Spirit wants to do through us.

A word about video . . .

Few media have affected *or infected* a generation more than television has in the last forty years. It has evolved from a simple novelty box to an indispensable centerpiece of the American family home. The average American will find time to spend 1/5 of their God-given life watching the infamous screen! With the possible exception of music, is there any greater common denominator among people in this nation? The question is: how will we implement video to reach pre-Christians?

For those who aren't sure how to get going in multimedia, here is a list of the basic components you'll need initially: video projector, screen, VCR, video camera, computer and software and a good consultant. Eventually you can add scanners, digital cameras, monitors, graphics, editing machines and more. Your constant goal in putting the equipment together is to produce video presentations that are seamless within themselves and within the context of the service. Productions that jump from scene to scene make it difficult for the audience to follow. It also draws more attention to the process. In order to do things effectively, it will take some funding at the outset. Don't automatically look for the cheapest equipment. You can be flexible, but as a rule, this isn't an area where you should be constantly looking for deals. Instead, hunt for quality, upgrade-ability and service. Fortunately, professional gear is getting less expensive all the time.

At SFC we commonly use our video screen to project items like announcements, digital slide shows of recent events tied to music, video clips of movies, live and pre-recorded on the street interviews, lyrics and message outlines, title slides for dramas and messages, pre-recorded testimonials, scanned images, children's choirs singing live from another part of our facility and background scenes. We've found it to be an extremely successful way to communicate to pre-Christians in our community.

Technology doesn't absolve us of authentic interaction with people. Because of the isolation that exists in our society, people are looking for meaningful relationships. P.T. Forsyth once said, "You must live with people to know their problems and live with God in order to help solve them."[2] Ministry is a relational process. Relational with God first, people second, and our gear and/or our performances following. As we become engrossed with equipment and technology, it becomes easy to spend large amounts of time researching, buying and learning new gear, while forgetting about the people who use it. It's easy to fall into the trap of thinking, "If I just had the best and latest gadget, then I could do ministry faster and more efficiently." Sometimes we get it backwards. People are the ministry. Although methods of communication and technology have changed dramatically over the years, ministry hasn't. Twenty-first century ministry really isn't any different than first, fourteenth or any other century's ministry.

Additions and deletions of new paradigm media/idea sources are always taking place, but here are a few current examples as we go to press.

Licensing Agencies:
* CCLI (Christian Copyright Licensing Incorporated), 800.234.2446.
* MPLC (Motion Picture Licensing Corporation), 800.462.8855.
* SWANK, 800.876.5577.
* Criterion, 800.890.9494.
* Motion Picture Association of America, 818.995.6600.

Churches:
* Coast Hills Community Church, Aliso Viejo, Cal., 714.362.0079, (www.coasthillschurch.org).
* Discovery Church, Orlando, Fla., 407.855.3140.
* Fellowship of Las Colinas, Dallas, Tex., (www.folc.org).
* Ginghamsburg Church, Tipp City, Ohio, 937.667.1069, (www.ginghamsburg.org).
* Saddleback Community Church, Lake Forest, Cal., (www.saddleback.com).
* Scottsdale Family Church, Scottsdale, Ariz., 602.614.0001, (www.primenet.com/~sfc).
* Willow Creek Community Church, S. Barrington, Ill., 847.765.0070, (www.willowcreek.org).

Books/Periodicals/Marketing:
* The Church Guide to Copyright Law Christian Ministry Resource, 704.841.8066.
* *The Source* (Resource book from Willow Creek for programming), Zondervan Publishing.
* *Out on the Edge*, by Michael Slaughter, Abingdon Press.
* *Christian Computing.*
* *Equip,* 303.665.8930.
* Fast Company, 800.688.1545, (www.fastcompany.com).
* *Inc.*, 800.234.0999, (www.inc.com).
* Technologies for Worship, 905.830.4300.
* *Worship Leader*, 800.286.8099.
* *On Mission*, (www.onmission.com).
* *Net Fax/NEXT,* 800.765.5323, (www.leadnet.org).
* *Outreach Marketing,* 760.940.0600, (www.outreachmarketing.com).
* *Details* (Marketing), 205.942.8055, (www.detailsmktg.com).
* *Manlove Communications,* (www.manlove.com).

Other Organizations:
- Creative Assistant (software for service programming), 813.392.6766.
- Gospel Communications Network (network of Christian resources), www.gospelcom.net.
- Leadership Network (organization developing leadership gifts), 800.765.5323.
- MC2 (resources for blended worship programming), 913.685.1377.
- Mission Media (video illustrations for sermons/commercials), 208.322.9090.
- *Taking Church Off Pause* (video and book series giving rationale and ideas for programming), 800.748.5119.
- TNT (The New Thing—a group of churches committed to new paradigm thinking and sharing ideas), 602.614.0001.
- Top Church Websites, www.topchurchwebsites.com).
- Visual Bible (the Bible on video, word for word, with a fresh presentation), 602.473.2323.
- Internet Movie Database, http://us.indb.com.
- Harbringer Communications (original video and slide presentations), 800.320.7206.

Television:
- The Edge (Weekly show airing on CNBC detailing new technology).

Conferences:
- Coast Hills Creative Communications Conference, 949.362.0079.
- Creative Church Conference, 972.257.8817, (www.folc.org).
- Inspirations Conference, 905.830.4300, (www.tfw.com).
- Willow Creek Leadership Conference, www.willowcreek.org).
- Saddleback Conference, 949.581.4248, (www.saddleback.com).
- Comdex, 617.449.6600.
- E3 (Electronic Entertainment Expo), www.mha.com/e3.
- Infocomm International, 800.659.SHOW, (www.infocom.org).
- MUSICalifornia, 818.993.8378.
- NAB (National Association of Broadcasters), 800.NAB.EXPO, (www.nab.org/conventions).
- NAMM (National Association of Music), 769.438.8001, (www.namm.com).

Drama and Arts Come to Church

For too long, the world has had a corner on the market for using the arts to convey its messages. Multiple billions of dollars are invested in advertising, entertainment, movies, television, publicity, acting, music, lighting, computer graphics, etc. While the Middle Ages and the Renaissance years tapped into the human potential for presenting the gospel via the arts, we lost this in later eras. While sanctifying the arts for use in the church is redemptive in nature, a deeper reason to pursue them is to communicate the gospel more effectively to a mediated culture. Here are five reasons to include the arts into your regular worship programming.

1. We need creative communication to reach a mediated culture. Most of us were raised around the television. From the boomers on, we have been inundated with complex, dynamic images both for entertainment and education. Because this is a part of our way of thinking, we need to understand how we can use these same tools to effectively communicate the gospel. Since the word *entertain* literally means to hold in tension, how can you convey a biblical truth if you do not entertain to a degree? People are not only used to multimedia, they expect it. The church need not relegate itself to the premedia era because it perceives this period to be more sacred.

2. Multimedia, drama, and dance engage our senses into our worship. Over the years, most of our holiness churches have lost a good amount of their emotion and passion during worship. We have become more cerebral in our services, assuming that a more dignified program somehow esteems God. As parents, we love our kids to get a bit gooey over us. Our heavenly Father loves the same. By engaging our senses and emotions, we open up the soul to hear and feel the truth of God which will transform it. Jesus told stories, visual illustrations which communicated complex concepts about the Kingdom. By using drama, dance, visual aids and media, we can go a step further in creating those visual pictures, which go far in conveying an important truth.

3. The arts often attract those who have been turned off by traditional churches. One of the main reasons new paradigm congregations are so effective at reaching the unchurched is often because they employ nontraditional means such as media and the arts to communicate the gospel. While the purpose of the arts is not purely for entertainment, many who are opposed to the "pipe organs and sermons only format", are apt to come again and again for creative communication such as drama vignettes, video clips, slide shows, and PowerPoint accents. Some people just need an excuse to give church another chance and many guests return due to new ways of communicating.

4. Media and the arts utilize the gifts of those often overlooked by the church. When we talk about lay ministry and participation, we often ignore those who have interest in the arts and/or audiovideo production. Music, drama, technical support and computer generation are all gifts and skills which can be used by God. By embracing these gifts, we help people understand how they can be sanctified for spiritual works of service to benefit the Body. When we ignore these gifts, we imply that God cannot use them and that there is little place for people so inclined in the Body. Most churches can significantly increase lay involvement by employing arts ministries.

5. Educating a post-Christian society requires multiple messages and media. When people had basic understanding of Christianity and the Bible, we could rely more on single or double forms, such as music and the spoken word. Post-Christian people do not have the same fundamentals and therefore require multiple images to construct the same concept. During the first few centuries, the Church created visual pictures such as the stations of the cross to educate the illiterate. Although most of our society is now literate, people's postmodern mind-set again requires us to move toward visual imagery to instill the stories of Christianity. Video clips, sketches, visual aides and pantomime are all powerful tools for making points which cannot be presumed among those who are biblically illiterate.

Utilize the arts appropriately. Services should be crafted holistically, striving to communicate a theme via the music, visuals and spoken word. I have seen drama and video clips used which seemed to convey no message and did not add to the sermon. The program directors did not seem to understand the importance of using the arts to gain attention and/or emphasize a point in the message. Occasionally we will use a vignette which is humorous but tied to the theme, just to engage attention and lighten the atmosphere prior to a heavy duty message. At other times, a pretty serious drama sketch can get the people ready to hear what God says about the situation. A sketch should avoid being preachy and having the answers neatly provided. Let it pique interest, engage attention, and illustrate the relevance of the theme to everyday life. The message will then provide God's answer and a biblical lesson on the theme.

Congregations which take the use of the arts seriously must realize that to do them well requires significant work and energy. Writing vignettes which illustrate message points, developing and training actors, rehearsing, and giving the final performance is a tedious process. There are numerous outlets for drama sketches, some in books and some online, but most need to be edited a bit to fit your style and/or a specific desired result in the service. The only thing worse than not using drama and the arts in church is to use them poorly. Mediocrity kills a service, so if a play or media effect is not done well, it should not be done at all. But don't let that stop you from doing something. Begin with the simple and work toward the more difficult. Never underestimate the effect of a short, simple dramatic reading or illustration to add significantly to a service.

ENDNOTES

[1]Lislie Ellis, *Jazz*, Sept. 1996.
[2]P.T. Forsyth, quote (source unknown)

Chapter 8

Leading with Wet Feet

by David A. Slamp

*T*here are few changes in ministry today that have impacted the inner lives and bonded progressive Wesleyans more than small group ministry. The value of groups was rediscovered in America during the 1980s and virtually every aggressive evangelical church today has some form of small group ministry. The transition today is from more traditional small groups centered around Bible study, toward including a community of 4-12 people in nearly every task-oriented group, often referred to as the metachurch. With this renewal have come a few objections and some major adjustments. For example, some don't understand why we need groups when it appears to them that Sunday school is a small group that meets the same needs. Others wrestle with how to keep all the services each week, plus adding this vital ministry. Still more are afraid of cliquishness and potential divisiveness. We tend to overestimate the spiritual formation that goes on in large group experiences and underestimate its importance in small groups, where there is accountability, individualized design, and relationship building. You cannot develop deep relationships during Sunday morning worship. We cannot assume that because we sit through countless sermons and large*

group Bible lessons, that we truly understand what it means to become salt and light and incarnations of Christ. Small groups help us dialogue and understand more closely what sermons look like when applied.

The old paradigm included small groups as an adjunct, add-on ministry. New paradigm ministries consider it a core value, expected of all members and active attendees. Our church in Scottsdale adheres to three primary values: 1) vibrant Sunday morning worship which allows believers to invite their unchurched friends: 2) every member ministry where we grow through the use of our spiritual gifts: and 3) spiritual formation via small groups. If we fail to communicate the importance and indispensability of small groups, they rarely take off. Unless we develop effective small group leaders, our church will be shallow in leadership and we will run the risk of divergent groups straying from the basics of our faith and promoting individual church philosophies of ministry. Small groups are important.

One of the experts on small groups in our movement is David Slamp. He is the associate pastor of small groups, discipleship and Christian education at Central Community Church (Church of God Anderson) in Wichita, Kansas. David understands and certainly believes in the importance of mini-congregations, which gather to provide pastoral care, teaching, discipleship, affirmation, encouragement, and friendship. He has a D. Min. in church growth from Fuller Theological Seminary, and is the author of CareRings *and* Small Groups that Work. *Married to Kathy, they have two grown children, Scott and Dana.*

Joshua and the priests of Israel demonstrated a transformation in leadership and ministry as they entered the Promised Land. Prior to their crossing the Jordan, Moses was the leader of the nation. Before him had been Joseph, Jacob, Isaac, and Abraham. God had always led Israel forward through one man.

But upon entering Canaan, the way God's people moved ahead changed. Joshua was still the leader but now the people, represented in the priests, were directly involved in moving ahead. This shift had begun in Exodus, chapter eighteen, when Moses conferred with Jethro about the work load. His father-in-law advised him to select others to help make decisions and lead the people. At Jericho, Joshua was not the up-front man. The **people** were. *The priests* carried the Ark of the Covenant. The

114

priests marched in front, and as soon as the toes of their sandals touched the Jordan, they were in God's land, Canaan. What God promised to the fathers individually, he gave to the sons collectively. They were actively involved in ministry. The people became leaders with wet feet.

While the priests in Joshua's day were the Levites, ordained of God to their role, today all true Christians are priests. The New Testament Church must involve lay people in smaller groups to move ahead in ministry and service. It's time we follow the advice of Jethro and identify with the experience at the Jordan. The Church will never move ahead to conquer the new land God has for us until pastors and people move through this transition and, like the priests of Joshua's day, become "leaders with wet feet." Small groups help people lead others spiritually to their new land.

Scores of progressive Wesleyan churches are discovering the power of this principle by getting their people involved in leading small groups. Skyline Wesleyan, for example, grew its Sunday school from 400 to 1200 in an eight-year period. During the last *two* years of that time, they caught the vision of small groups and their groups grew from zero to over 1,400. New Hope in Portland and Central Community in Wichita, Kansas, have grown dramatically with the use of small groups. These churches were led by Wesleyan pastors who caught the vision of training leaders to "get their feet wet" by leading small groups. More than anyone, Wesleyans should embrace the concept of small groups, since the Class Meetings are an integral part of our heritage.

Small groups provide many more arenas for lay ministry to take place. Rick Warren writes,

> "You don't judge an army's strength by how many people sit in the mess hall. You judge an army on the basis of how many people are trained and active on the front line. The percentage of members being mobilized for ministry . . . is a more reliable indicator of health than how many people attend services."[1]

Obstacles and Objections

As I speak to pastors and lay leaders in various denominations, I am amazed how often the same questions arise: 1) Why are groups needed? I'm in Sunday school. Isn't that a small group? 2) Aren't groups dangerous? Can't they become cliquish or places for theological and even political disagreements? 3) Aren't people too busy to be in a small group? They have Sunday school, worship, Sunday evening, and Wednesday.

Aren't small groups just like Sunday schools? In the majority of cases, Sunday school classes are set up and taught in ways that actually *keep them* from operating like small groups. The only similarity is that sometimes they have 10 to 12 in attendance. Most classes are set up with students in rows and a teacher who stands at a lectern. Often not trained in leading discussion, teachers use the lecture method for their classes. Consequently, many class discussions are basically a sharing of stories and opinions on the topic of the week. This setting hardly constitutes a small group. Groups are informal. They include significant times of prayer, life application of the Word, and (perhaps most importantly) are led by a thoroughly trained leader who also gives care to those in need and follows up on absentees.

Healthy small groups avoid cliquish behavior and gossip. When leaders are untrained, when there is no supervision, when those in charge don't know how to equip lay leaders, gossip and cliques may exist. None of these problems need to develop. The key is to carefully select and thoroughly train leaders, monitoring their progress and dealing with problems as they arise. Most churches already have cliques in them whether or not we recognize it. I would rather train and equip members to lead—and then monitor their progress for spiritual purposes—than to let groups develop at random without guidance, prayer and leadership training. We must make the shift to embrace lay ministry and care-giving. Small groups offer the ideal instrument for both.

The toughest objection is the third question: *"Aren't people too busy to be in a small group? They have Sunday school, worship, Sunday evening and Wednesday."* The answer is, "Yes, they are too busy." We must concentrate on the most effective approaches to the gospel. We must see that the value of offering support and encouragement weekly to our people outweighs less effective events and programs. Choose a productive method and ministry over a stale ministry of the church. Effective pastors make the decision to lead their people to be disciplers. In a small group ministry, every absentee can be contacted and lay people can be developed as spiritual leaders. Informal settings meet a profound need for intimacy in our day. Creating small groups and empowering our people to minister may mean dropping a service that is neither growing nor spiritually significant.

To cut existing ministries is a tough decision. Such a decision must be made on the basis of solid biblical principles and priorities, not because of our traditions. It must be made kindly, with focused patience and with the blessing of our church leaders. But we must move on!

The bottom line to objections about small groups involves a major shift in our thinking and the way we minister. We start seeing people as ministers, pastors, and as equippers of the saints for the work of ministry, as instructed in Ephesians, chapter four. This means pastors do more teaching, training, leading, encouraging and equipping of lay leaders and less frontline ministry. Pastors will still minister and lead, but in a different, more efficient way. Lay leaders will be getting their feet wet in a different arena of ministry: equipping others. They will be getting *their feet wet* ministering to many more than they could ever reach themselves!

Why We Must Move Ahead

In *Turn Around Churches*, George Barna calls pastors to visionary leadership. "Stalwarts in a dying church often argue that things will return to normal if the church can do a better job of doing what it has always done."[2] The opposite is true. Evangelism and church growth mean turning our backs on the way we used to do them, taking a fresh look at needs today and setting out to meet those needs in ways that fit this age. That requires vision. Barna writes, "Without vision, there is no reason to change. Without leadership, there is no path upon which change can be managed intelligently."[3] There are at least four reasons why we must change our thinking and approach to groups:

First, we must move ahead because the universal priesthood of believers is real. All God's people can bring others to Him in intercessory prayer and offer themselves "as living sacrifices, holy and pleasing to God . . ." (Rom. 12:1). All Christians are priests. That means that all can serve and minister. If the pastor has to do it all, the church will grow about as fast as one person can work. When everyone is unleashed as a minister, a church will grow beyond the best pastor's lone efforts.

Second, far too many Wesleyan heritage churches are either declining or just not reaching and evangelizing the lost. To aggressively pursue the unchurched and turn this trend around, we must spot effective means of reaching seekers on their turf. Many pastors and churches today assume that to check the decline, they must add more items to the already full calendar, with little thought of efficacy. They build one program on top of another, hoping that somehow they will be more effective, when actually they are becoming less efficient. Our need is to select fruitful approaches to ministry like small groups and lead them well.

Third, we must live out what we believe and preach—that people are saved and filled with God's Holy Spirit in order to reach a lost world. We have God's promise from Acts 1:8 that when the Holy Spirit

117

comes upon us we will be witnesses. In Acts 2:46 and 20:20, the church met to pray, fellowship and worship in homes. There is a direct link between being filled with the Spirit and witnessing. Whether it was Jesus being crucified, Stephen being stoned, the Apostle Paul or Peter being persecuted—as long as they were filled, they told the good news.

Reaching the lost implies we must stretch. In the Great Commission we are told to go to the unchurched with the gospel. In Luke 14:23 Jesus instructs us to compel or encourage the lost to come to Him. We are told to go to them. This means stretching out to reach them. A further value of small groups is that they get to where the lost are—to homes in their neighborhoods. Rather than asking seekers to come to us, we will be going to where they live. With certain small groups, we can get the good news to people who have been hurt at a church or who would never come into our sanctuaries because of guilt over their sins, shame for their past, or a fear of the unknown or guilt for their past or sins.

Fourth, the world is crying out and literally dying for intimacy and relationships. Living in a technological world with impersonal communication such as the TV, fax, computer, and phone, people long for relationships. We visit the World Wide Web, but don't know the names of our next door neighbors. Sesame Street and MTV raise our children. An office worker may sit at a computer all day, but never once talk with a friend. "Today, in America, people are losing their ability to interact without the help of some institution like the church."[4] As a result, people are missing connectedness and relationships. This phenomenon has given us a golden opportunity. The church is faced with a remarkable opportunity to fill the "relationship void." In this climate, the personal touch of groups can make a profound impact on people's lives.

Seeing it as a passing fad, some are saying the day of small groups is over. In 1996, George Barna stated that groups are declining. In some churches that is true. If we don't work them, they won't work! In every church I know where small groups have not grown, the reason can be found in one of three areas mentioned: vision, training, and/or effort. Many pastors start with the best of intentions, but do not follow through. They don't stay with small groups long enough for them to be effective. The only groups that don't work are those that are not worked. The long-term result of shifting from program to program is that our people become confused and wary of anything new, knowing it probably will not last.

Realistic Solutions

When there is an effective training program in place for small groups, it is amazing how few problems arise. Although we have over 50 small groups involving over 600 people in the church where I serve, we have very few problems. Part of the reason for this is that to be a Shepherd (our name for a small group leader) one must complete three elements of training. We require that every small group leader receive five to seven hours of intensive training, many weeks of participation and observation in groups, and a signed covenant. Candidates must also read a text, *Small Groups that Work.* Quality training is extremely important. There are many ways people can be equipped for ministry. Small group training simply equips them to be effective leading others to Christ and making disciples.

Of the thirty churches studied by George Barna that have literally turned around from declining to thriving congregations, the common denominator was that the pastor equipped the people for ministry. Barna states,

> . . . turnaround pastors gave top priority to *equipping the laity for effective, targeted ministry.* Indeed, until the people believed enough in themselves as ministers on God's behalf, there was little chance that they would believe the church could sustain a comeback.[5]

We must focus on this need. Many of our lay people love God dearly. They give unselfishly and believe wholeheartedly in the church and its ministry. But they have not been challenged to minister. Carl George was asked whether it was more important to develop a strong leadership base or small groups. George's reply was that building a strong leadership base is certainly the more important concern. He went on to say that it just so happens the most effective and productive way to build a leadership base is through small groups.

Far too often, pastors go to seminars and conferences, are stirred by a concept, take it home, only to see it fall flat as they present it to their leadership team or church board. The key for training today is to develop teams of pastors and lay leaders. In seminars I teach, we invite every pastor to have at least 8 to 10 lay leaders with him at the seminar. I believe in the lay-driven church. That is what the most influential and effective churches have always been, whether the lay involvement took the form of witnessing, Sunday school, or even a financial campaign. When lay men and women are trained, empowered, and entrusted with authority, God blesses it. Let all the priests get their feet wet!

119

Small groups work best when they are a ministry, not a program.
A small groups program is a common reason why groups do not last in a given church. Traditional pastors throw programs at needs. New paradigm pastors know the *purpose* behind a ministry. They are open and responsive, but want to know the church is not just jumping through another hoop. Approaching small groups as a program saps people of their vitality. Programs make small groups an end in themselves rather than a means to the end of reaching the lost and discipling the "found."

In order to make small groups a means to an end, establish them as an integral part of other ministries. Include group time as *a part of* the ushers' service, Sunday school teachers, or other ministry teams. David Boots, pastor of the music and worship arts ministries at Central Community, has divided the 160-voice choir into small discipleship groups of 10 to 12. Leaders call or contact absentees, send appreciation notes, birthday and anniversary cards. This strategy keeps groups from being another program. The key is communities; not committees. Follow-up and care are provided naturally. I have seen many children's workers grow "weary in well doing." They do not attend their own Sunday school class. Many children's church workers give up attending the worship service. Children's pastors often miss both. Even more, some of them oversee a midweek children's night. How can we nourish our caregivers? Form CareRings (our name for small groups) among the workers in each department. We structure quality time for spiritual development and relationship building by scheduling a small group activity as a part of every ministry role in the church. If we'll think about it, there are dozens of creative ways to add caregiving to our ministry schedule.

Another twist on this idea is to consider small groups as ministry groups. Barb Feese, the leader of one of our CareRings, called to ask if her CareRing could adopt a pastor. They wanted to find a deserving pastor of some small church nearby to care for at Christmas. What a powerful idea. A ministry task helps group members remember that they are not in CareRings for themselves, but for others. Another CareRing makes breakfast one Saturday morning each month for about 30 people in our church who do service projects in the community.

People need to be needed. With training, they are willing to serve. As they are empowered to lead and minister, most people thrive in ministry. They appreciate being part of a ministry team, of belonging.

The CareRing ministry can also be used to respond to the objections of being too busy. While at Nashville First Nazarene, I was given the opportunity and challenge to develop a small group ministry. That traditional church has a very strong Sunday school. As I began researching how to begin a small group ministry, I did not want to organize it in such a way as to compete with Sunday school. I read every book on groups I could, listened to dozens of tapes, attended two small group conferences, and visited three or four churches with small groups ministries. No one I could find knew of any resources that could tell me how to start groups in churches with healthy Sunday schools.

After about three months of research, I had the idea of making groups part of Sunday school. Many people I talked to wanted to build relationships. Most of them wanted to grow spiritually and were willing to devote some time doing so. We approached the adult Sunday school classes about the idea. They responded well. We wrote training materials and set up training. Within the first six months, we had 14 groups.[6]

Let CareRings be the way classes provide discipleship and care to their people. A coworker of mine has proven this as an effective means of growth. Bob Beckler, pastor of Involvement at Central Community, teaches a dynamic Sunday school class. When he came on staff just over a year ago, he studied the CareRing manual and committed to building his class with small groups. The class was averaging about 30 to 40 and had three CareRings. A year later, they have seven CareRings and the class is averaging over 110. The class has moved into a new room twice for more space. These class members are all young adults with families of two or three grade schoolers. Bob has proven to everyone that even very busy people are ready for groups when they are presented positively and consistently. Groups meet needs.

Groups are stronger when they focus on spiritual formation rather than being Bible studies. Biblical knowledge is essential to spiritual growth, but the point here is that Bible study should not be an end in itself. Our primary objective is *not* Bible knowledge. The highest purpose of our ministry is to apply truth to our lives so that we might become mature and fully devoted disciples. We need to keep our eyes on spiritual development, more than on fellowship, bonding, Bible knowledge, and so on. Every one of these is important, just not the most essential.

We need to take a variety of approaches to groups. At Central we have **CareRings** of 10 to 12 participants who meet weekly in homes for about 1½ hours for caregiving, prayer support, and application of the Bible. They may meet for a number of months or even years, but always have a purpose to start new groups. Four or five **Support Groups** meet each week for such special needs as weight loss, substance abuse and divorce recovery. These tend to be larger and are more oriented to caregiving of specific needs. They are led by highly trained men and women, many of whom have suffered some loss, divorce, addiction, etc. **Gap Groups** are for middle school students. These 13 groups meet for 45 minutes every Wednesday at the church following an activity time and teaching. **Special Interest Groups** include Crown Ministry (small groups for financial management) and other needs such as parenting, caring for aged parents, etc. These are less intense than Support Groups, and meet normally from 3 to 6 months. **Ministry Related Groups** are connected with a ministry like those mentioned above. All a bit different, they take on the personality of their ministry area. **Discipleship Groups** (DG) hold members accountable and consist of only 2 to 4 members of the same gender. DGs meet from 6 to 9 months for an hour each week. The express, unique purpose of Discipleship Groups is to train up a disciple who in turn will lead one to four others. Leading our fellowships through change takes skill and patience. Draw on the type of group or groups that meet the needs in your church. Your congregation is unique, so the approach to groups must fit it, not duplicate what is done elsewhere.

Practical Ideas

There are a number of practical guidelines that will help us begin a small group ministry or develop an existing one. Start in prayer. Nothing is more essential than this. Pray as a pastor or staff member and lead your leaders to join you in prayer for God's direction. Let Him lead you to believe whether or not groups are for your church. The power of this is that if God leads you to start, you can let others know it is from Him! Start with what I call the real leaders. These are not those elected to the official church board. Some not on the board exert a profound influence.

Begin where your church is. Evaluate what its needs are. Carefully think through whether or not there are special needs. Some churches have a lot of blended families. Others have a high jobless rate. Still others may have people who want to work on losing weight, substance control, or even raising junior highers. Groups can be formed around these types of concerns.

You may not have a plan for building up fully devoted disciples in your fellowship. Your ministry may consist of Sunday school and three church services a week. You may not be offering groups for accountability and mentoring. The best place to start is where you are now. Since groups naturally form and expand along relationship lines, begin with existing networks such as Sunday school classes. Those people already see each other weekly. They know first names. Offer CareRings or similar ministry to them as a class. Later, expand what you offer to include support groups, discipleship, accountability groups, or others. Remember, we are experiencing a leadership shift, from pastor-centered to lay-centered ministry. It may be scary to pastors. Start with your most faithful and teachable leaders. You may need to relieve them of committee work and let go of less productive busywork. Trust God to show you what needs to go and then *let go!*

Once the pastor and the leaders agree it is time to begin a small group ministry, find someone to coach you through the process. Bring together the real leaders and potential small group leaders to hear an expert on small groups teach the strategy and methods for an initial training day. Their enthusiasm will be contagious. They will have the answers to some of the toughest questions people may have.

Allow the laity to minister and lead. Train them and trust them. Let them become what they were meant to be—**"Leaders with Wet Feet!"** Then let God lead. He will enable you to have a small group ministry that builds healthy, mature disciples. They will minister to others and help them get their feet wet. Monitor their progress. Encourage them and pray for them. Stay close, but let them go. They are *priests*. What a great day is ahead for our churches when God leads, when pastors become equippers of the saints, and when the people take spiritual responsibility. Let the priests do it. ***Let them put their toes in the water and cross into Canaan!***

ENDNOTES

[1]Rick Warren, "Comprehensive Health Plan," *Leadership Journal*, Vol. xviii, No. 3 (Summer, 1997), p. 24.

[2]George Barna, *Turn Around Churches*, (Ventura, Cal.: Regal Books, 1993), p. 37.

[3]Ibid., p. 37.

[4]Ibid., p. 85.

[5]Ibid., p. 49.

[6]David A. Slamp, *CareRings, A Small Group Ministry Designed to Enhance Your Sunday School*, (Forrest, Va.: Church Growth Institute, 1995). This small group training packet was developed in a local church to provide leaders with practical instruction where groups are developed to coordinate the Sunday School.

Chapter 9

Excellence— Overcoming the Lake Wobegon Effect

by Glenn Teal

"*A*nd God saw everything that He had created and noted it was good" (paraphrase). God's good is our great. The concepts of quality control and total quality management did not originate with Deming, but are a part of biblical theology. Those of us in the holiness movement should understand the concept of excellence as much as anyone—moral and spiritual quality. God calls for the unblemished lamb, first fruits, and total commitment. Jesus turned water into the best wine. Yet, when it comes to ministry, church buildings, and services, so many people of faith assume that second best is okay. Somehow, we presume that since we're a 501.3C charitable organization, we should settle for hand-me-downs and leftover time and talents.*

Schaller said that just as the 60s, 70s and 80s were noted for church growth, the key to the 90s and the first part of the 21st century is quality. We cannot scrimp on quality and hope people will come and get involved in our churches. People used to put up with chipped paint and moldy carpet in the children's classrooms, missing notes in Sunday's solo, and dry, boring messages from the pulpit. Today's discriminating church shopper seeks excellence. We may not think it fair to be judged with the likes of for-profit groups, but like it or not, that's the reality today. What we need to do is thank our culture for forcing us to raise our standards. The Bible says that whatever we do, do it as unto the Lord. Shabby landscaping, smudged worship folders, antiquated clipart, and unpolished worship services won't cut it in the 21st century. Too often we've confused low self-esteem for humility. Too often we've assumed that uninvolved people were not spiritual, when in reality they were too ashamed to be associated with us, let alone ask their friends and neighbors to visit our church. Excellence is often confused with pride and wastefulness, which need not be the case. Sloppy agape won't make it in the future. New paradigm congregations know that quality counts and it is much more a mind-set than a price tag. Mediocrity costs more than quality. People aren't drawn to attend or give money to things which are poorly done.

One leader who has had a burden for quality is Glenn Teal, a Canadian under whose ministry the LakeView Free Methodist Church in Saskatoon became the largest Free Methodist Church in Canada. He is a graduate of Spring Arbor College in Michigan and Western Evangelical Seminary (now part of George Fox University) in Oregon. With his wife, Nancy, and children, Alexander and Angela, Glenn now pastors at CrossRoads Community Church, a contemporary and fast-growing Free Methodist congregation in Temperance, Michigan, a Michigan suburb of Toledo, Ohio.

Achieving excellence in ministry is both exciting and difficult. Excellence honors God and inspires people, but it also demands a high price, a price that begins with honest self-evaluation. How many times have you heard worship leaders imply that their church services are the next best thing to the Crystal Cathedral, only to visit them and discover a poorly planned, under-rehearsed, and sloppily led service featuring instrumentalists who play badly, singers who sang off-key, and speakers who didn't connect with the congregation? Too often we insist that everything in our church is "just great, thanks," when in reality the children and youth programs are second-rate, facilities are unkept and the administrative structure is in chaos. Whenever we take comfort by telling ourselves that we're doing better than average, when in reality we're not, who are we kidding? Usually only ourselves.

Church leaders are not alone in this self-delusional thought pattern. The average American thinks he is above average. This self overestimation is so common that master marketer Harry Beckwith has named it "The Lake Wobegon Effect."[1] Garrison Keillor, PBS radio personality, says that people who live in his mythical hometown of Lake Wobegon, Minnesota are convinced that "all the women are strong, all the men are good looking, and all the children are above average." Far too many congregations are mired in mediocrity, but keep telling themselves differently. The Lake Wobegon Effect impairs our vision. It is time to honestly tell the truth about the quality of our ministry and then seek God's help to change. Besides, who ever said that God would be satisfied with just average ministries and churches anyway? Doesn't God call us to something higher?

God's Call to Excellence

God calls His people to live lives and build ministries which are marked by excellence. This call grows out of the very essence of God's character. "He is the Rock, his works are perfect, and all his ways are just" (Deut. 32:4). "As for God, his way is perfect; the word of the LORD is flawless." (Ps. 18:30) We are called to follow "the most excellent way" (1 Cor 12:31) and to think about those things which are "excellent or praiseworthy" (Phil. 4:8). Yet too often we aspire to excellence of heart while we settle for mediocrity in ministry.

The road to excellence should have a special appeal for those of us in the Wesleyan holiness heritage who for years have taken seriously God's call to holy living. We teach that God's perfection spurs us on to seek perfect love. It's time we take God's call to emulate His excellence in the way we do ministry seriously? Certainly, our Lord's call to "be perfect, therefore, as your heavenly Father is perfect" (Matt. 5:48) has far-reaching implications for the way we do church!

In addition to heeding the call of God, we must also connect with lost people in today's culture. People expect excellence in everything from their morning coffee (latte or cappuccino) to the late night news. Surrounded by a "quality is job one" culture, we've grown to expect the best. Fast food chains now deliver "spotless restrooms and world class french fries in 50 seconds for 79 cents."[2] What about the church? What do we deliver with excellence?

New paradigm churches have leaders who understand that mediocrity often jams the communication channels between the gospel message and our unchurched neighbors. Generally, churched people are reluctant to pursue excellence (too demanding) while at the same time our unchurched friends perceive that all things churchy are mediocre. Lost people deserve the best, but expect the worst. It is time to leave the comfortable, self-delusional patterns of the "Lake Wobegon Effect" and pursue the higher calling of the "Excellence Endeavor." Satisfaction with being average or above, must give way to a new holy passion to be excellent.

To Tell the Truth

Like the TV game show of the late 60s, it's time "To Tell the Truth." Church leaders, pastors and others need to be the first truth tellers—even if it hurts. Unless we are willing to hear the truth and tell the truth about our music program, our children's and youth ministries, even the quality of our preaching, we will not improve.

When was the last time you and other leaders in your ministry honestly evaluated the key areas of your church? Who helped with the evaluation? What standards and measurements were applied? Did you dare tell yourself the truth? If we do not intentionally evaluate the quality of our ministries, we will unintentionally be and do less than our best.

Over the past 10 years in the two congregations I have led, we made a deliberate decision to become more honest in our self-evaluation. We asked ourselves the tough questions. Everyone, including myself, signed on for regular evaluations. Egos were put aside for the greater good of giving God our very best. At LakeView Free Methodist Church in Saskatoon, Canada, we contracted with a church consultant to do a formal evaluation of every aspect of our ministry. His comments produced a wealth of valuable information. Our publications were too simple and infrequent. We assumed that most people were in church most Sundays and relied far too heavily on our bulletin to communicate information. On our consultant's recommendation we implemented redundant communication, repeating the same message over and over in several media. We added a newsletter, printed in a local print shop for better graphics and greater exposure, and completely updated the weekly bulletin.

Many other improvements came from acting upon our consultant's report. Offices expanded, ministry schedules adjusted, and administrative structures reorganized. We even redecorated the ladies' rooms. In the course of three months, we took several small and large steps toward a higher standard of excellence. It was one thing to hire a consultant, it was another to accept his critique and follow through on his recommendations. Whether or not you hire a church consultant, it is incredibly important to make a commitment to gain honest feedback about your ministry.

At CrossRoads, we evaluate our ministry in several ways. We send evaluation cards to our visitors. More important, we take their observations seriously by passing them down to ministry directors and asking them to act on each suggestion as quickly as possible. Our staff often ask newcomers for honest first impressions and suggestions. Like the long-time resident who no longer notices the chipped paint on the foyer walls, most church leaders become oblivious to our church's shortcomings over time. We need to find a way to see things through fresh eyes, either by hiring consultants, inviting evaluation, or by asking an honest colleague to observe and then critique some aspect of our ministry.

Tough Questions

Every six months or so, we review the following questions with our key team members: boards, pastors and lay ministry leaders.

1. What would it take to move this ministry toward greater excellence?
2. How can we improve what is now acceptable in this ministry, so that it becomes very good?
3. If some aspects of this ministry are far from excellent—should we suspend them until we can do a more God-honoring job?
4. What simple things could we do in the next 30 days to improve the quality of our: music, nursery, facilities (outside and inside), printed materials, youth and children's programs, teaching and preaching?

Someone takes notes. Assignments are made and deadlines set. Individuals take responsibility and, as senior pastor, I hold people accountable.

Affirm the Small Stuff

In our passion for excellence, it is often difficult to remember to affirm every positive step along the way. For those of us in volunteer-intensive ministry, we must master the fine art of catching people doing something right. Our conversations need to include phrases such as: "Hey, that was terrific! The whole team got it right this time! Keep it up! Great job everybody!" This is a huge challenge because once we are committed to excellence, there are times when it is difficult to affirm improved, but still imperfect performance. We want to hold out for better performance.

Unless we affirm moderate improvements, the motivation for higher standards will be lost. Most people will try even harder if their initial efforts are recognized and appreciated.

Leadership with Vulnerability

In addition to hiring a consultant and organizing teams for evaluation, our staff also carries out weekly ministry evaluations. Every week we discuss new ways to improve on our ministry performance. This takes leadership. On his tape "Delighting God with Excellence," Bill Hybels quotes Peter Drucker as saying that "leadership is about the setting and the enforcing of standards."[3] It's a tough job. But if the pastor doesn't champion the call to excellence, who will?

Senior pastors can never exclude themselves from the evaluation process if they expect to improve. Twice a year I call together a select group of influencers in our church to talk about my preaching. Over the course of a morning or afternoon session, we brainstorm new ideas for upcoming series that will better connect with real people in our community.

In the course of the day, both positive and negative comments are made about previous messages. It is very important to the process that I encourage the feedback and respond in a gracious and nondefensive manner. It isn't always easy, but it is the right thing to do. People can tell when leaders are too self-protective to hear the truth about themselves. They also know if we are able take some loving correction. As the point person, a pastor must invite honest evaluation and take it graciously if the process is to succeed.

Find Some Models

What does excellence look like? Many of us have done our thing the same way for so long, we think we've got it nailed, when in fact we are slipping. In our fast-paced world, the standards of excellence are constantly being raised, even in church work. The "same ol' same ol'" just won't cut it!

Both in Canada and now in Michigan, our churches have networked with other congregations who were models of excellence. Whether you make connections with the Willow Creek Association or The New Thing network or a dynamic growing church nearby, exciting opportunities are available. The leaders of strong churches in your area would welcome the chance to encourage you and your ministry. Call someone at Woodale Church in Minneapolis or Pearce Memorial Free Methodist near

Rochester, New York, or Skyline Wesleyan in San Diego, California. Ask for a copy of their Sunday bulletin and newsletter. Request information on staff meetings or leadership structures. They will be happy to help, as would most of the authors who are contributing to this book.

Concepts Not Details

As you network, don't look for details to copy as much as concepts and ideas that might be adaptable in your setting. You will soon realize that new standards of excellence are being set every day all over the country. Not long ago, TNT sent me a copy of the brochure produced by Skyline Wesleyan for its recent stewardship campaign. In two minutes, my understanding of excellence in printing was seriously revised.

New Standards

At CrossRoads, we've realized that photocopied invitations don't cut it; color printing does. Improvised offertories, under-rehearsed dramas, and underprepared worship times are not good enough. Our worship band practices five hours a week and the singers three hours a week together, in addition to personal practice time. Sound and light technicians set up at least two hours before each service. Each week the drama team practices the script for the next Sunday as well as the one scheduled a week later.

Saturday night specials—those late night, thrown-together messages—may get me through in a crisis, but they are not acceptable week to week. Currently, I average twelve hours of dedicated sermon preparation time, writing and rewriting, in addition to my general reading and study time. During the months leading up to Christmas and Easter, when I memorize the messages entirely, preparation time doubles.

Invest More than Money

Moving toward excellence does not necessarily mean spending a fortune. Since CrossRoads is not a megachurch with an enormous budget, we cannot make every improvement we'd like. We can strategically allocate time and resources to those ministries that will yield the greatest Kingdom return. We ask ourselves: Which ministries are reaching new people? What simple things can we do right away to make them more effective?

Excellence isn't just throwing more money at our weak places. It is making the commitment to do the very best to honor God with what we have. Our facilities may not be lavish, but they can be sparkling clean.

Our children's programs may not be high-tech, but they can be both entertaining and enlightening. Our music may not be perfect, but it is carefully planned, well-rehearsed and prayerfully offered. Our preaching may not be more imaginative than Max Lucado's, but it can be creative and compelling.

Excellence Honors God and Inspires People

Excellence honors God and inspires people. The bias of many if not most unchurched visitors is that their venture into religious life will be shoddy and second-class. For many newcomers, excellence in landscaping, music, facilities, and messages comes as a pleasant surprise. For some, a commitment to excellence is a kind of common ground that can earn us and the gospel a second hearing.

Lee Strobel, a teaching pastor at Willow Creek Community Church, tells of the sense of "commonality" he felt as an atheist attending his first services at Willow Creek. The passion and quality evident throughout the service was for him "a point of connection and even inspiration."[4] Pursuing excellence in your weekly Sunday services can increase your evangelistic effectiveness. That alone should inspire us to a greater passion for excellence in worship.

Excellence, Yes! Perfectionism, No!

The kind of God-inspired passion for excellence we are advocating is not to be confused with a compulsive obsession with perfectionism. No church will thrive if its people are constantly driven to reach for unattainable levels of flawlessness that burn people out. In ministry, as in all of life, minor errors are understandable. Healthy leaders realize this. Compulsive leaders can discourage volunteers and dishonor God, just as a careless leader. Every person and program has limits. But grace giving is no excuse for poor planning and sloppy ministry. Set a high enough standard to honor God, motivate our congregation, and inspire all who participate in our ministry.

Private Contract with God

Excellence in ministry begins in the heart of the leader. We need an inner motivation to honor God which grows out of a private covenant with Him. The passion necessary to keep a ministry functioning at a high level of excellence cannot be self sustained. We each need regular encounters with a holy God that compel us to offer everything we have in exchange for His unspeakable gift.

We might be able to get by with mediocrity in ministry, but after all Christ has done for us—why would we want to? When the leader models a personal passion for excellence that grows out of a heart full of love for God, then he has the moral authority to call the entire endeavor to the same kind of commitment.

Breaking free from the Lake Wobegon Effect and committing ourselves to the Excellence Endeavor are crucial. Not only does God deserve it—our church and community are dying for it. In fact, many are dying for lack of it.

ENDNOTES

[1]Harry Beckwith, *Selling the Invisible* (New York: Warner Books, 1997), pp. 5, 6.
[2]Ibid., p. 7.
[3]Bill Hybels, *Defining Moments Audiocassette: Delighting God with Excellence* (Grand Rapids: Zondervan Publishing House, 1996), Tape #23.
[4]Ibid.
(See also Alan Nelson and Stan Toler's book on excellence called *The 5 Star Church* by Regal Books.)

Chapter 10

Transitioning a Rural Church

by Dwight Mason

eing raised on a Midwest farm, I attended country and small-town churches through junior high school. For those of us separated by so many miles of dirt and gravel roads, these were significant centers for cultural development and friendship building. One year while in college, I worked for a farmer near the school in order to defray my tuition. As a senior I must have seemed a bit smug about my education, because during a conversation I asked the farmer if he had ever gone to college. "Yes, I've completed my doctorate in economics except for my dissertation." "Oh, that's great," I responded humbly. I realized back then that my stereotype of the simple, backward farmer was itself backward and simplistic. Having traveled back home a few times over the years, I have seen the dilapidated schools, the vacant farm houses, and the changing environment of rural America.

While a growing percentage of people live in and around urban centers, a large number of churches still minister in and around rural communities. Some prophetically suggest that these are bastions of resistance to change and monolithic has-beens. But a growing number of versatile pastors are recognizing that times are changing for the rural church and that many of our stereotypes of non-urban people are dated.

For the leader who sees with new eyes, the opportunities arise. The story is told of two shoe salesmen who went to Africa. One called home and said "I'm coming back. No one wears shoes over here." The other wired, "Send all you've got; nobody has any yet!" Regardless of the culture, people love excitement and hope. Pastors with vision can transform rural churches into vibrant communities of faith which at times can attract more attenders than the hosting town's actual population, as is being reported in burgs around the nation.

As times in rural America have changed, so must our churches. Dwight Mason is one man doing what so many others claim is impossible, transforming a formerly sleepy rural church into a dynamic, exciting community of faith. Dwight is the senior pastor of Sugarcreek Free Methodist Church in Ohio. A 1983 graduate of Circleville Bible College, he was appointed to Sugarcreek in 1985, when the church ran around 75 in attendance. The church now is running nearly 700 in Sunday morning worship. Dwight is married to Patty and is dad to Caleb, Sarah, and Jonathan.

Sugarcreek, Ohio is a warm and bustling little community nestled in the hills of Amish country. The Cleveland Browns football team was a Sugarcreek favorite for years, metropolitan Cleveland being a reasonable distance for real football fans to travel. The quarterback most closely identified with the Browns was Bernie Kosar. Picked in the expansion draft, he had publicly declared his choice and desire to be a member of the Cleveland Browns. This kind of choice had not happened in a long time in Cleveland. For many years, Cleveland had been a "pass through" for professional athletes, either coming or going as a last resort. Kosar believed he could help Cleveland win championships. When he was selected, a fast bond immediately developed between Bernie and the people of Cleveland. He was there by choice. He wanted to be there. He believed together they could win. The Browns and Bernie had years of a winning, fulfilling championship relationship.

The first key to ministry success in a rural community is similar: the confidence of God's call and joy in being there. When I was appointed to this rural congregation, I only accepted the appointment because I had received a specific call from God to this area. I repeatedly shared with my core congregation that I *chose* Sugarcreek. I was not coming just for a while to sharpen my skills in preparation for a larger, more prestigious work. I was committed to being pastor there as long as I could envision. Too often, career-orientation takes over and small churches are seen as stepping stones to a bigger, better, more honorable place. This seems to be the attitude of many who come to pastor a rural church. I affirmed again and again that our relationship would be like a good marriage: there would be times when we disagreed and even felt anger at each other, but I made the commitment that I would not run and I trusted they would not either. We would work together and this would be our church. God's call for me to be the pastor of this specific, rural church was strong. I had a burning desire to lead a ministry that would permeate the community, not just maintain and sustain the current situation. My passion for what could be, my certainty of God's call, and my sense of joy and pride at pastoring this particular church set the environment for partnership success. The first key to ministry success in a rural community is the confidence of God's call and joy in being there.

Most success stories in business or ministry have inspiring, progressive leadership as a common thread. The rural church is no exception. The church's pastor must be progressive personally, thinking and acting in a manner that sets a standard for the church in its own eyes and in the perception of the community. A neighbor of our church facility expressed surprise at my consistent arrival at the church early in the morning. "Pastors here usually don't go in until 11 o'clock or so," he laughed. In rural areas, the pastor is commonly seen as a buddy, a good old boy. Relationships are very important, but the effective rural pastor's primary identification must be as a man or woman of God, a strong leader, who can lead and who will give direction to the abundant life.

The pastor must look for opportunities and quickly set the tone for change and progress. I see several crucial decisions over the years that involved personal risk, sacrifice, and discernment.

1. The church's sound system was ancient and was more of a distraction than a help. The speakers were car speakers in a covered box. The first Sunday I had the service, I sang a solo with a taped accompaniment. I am not a great singer, but this was something new to our congregation and signaled a new day. I obtained a personal loan and purchased a sound system for the church, illustrating my commitment to excellence and progress in ministry.

2. Within three months, I shared with the Leadership Team some of the straw men we would face as we began to be the church our community needed. Regularly we faced our fears and addressed the

questions of the congregation. One fear was that becoming a large church would not allow us to know everyone. We had an icebreaker one evening to address this. Each person on the team was to share something about the person next to them that was personal, something not generally known that they had learned by spending quality time with them. This was a very difficult experience. As we shared, we discovered that in our little church we really did not know much about each other, and that whether you are in a big church or a little church, you become just about as close as you determine to be.

3. I prioritized people. My discretionary time during the work week always went to people. I ate breakfast, lunch, played racquetball, and took trips. I did everything I could think of to build relationships. It's rare for people to buy what you're selling if they don't like you. It's also unnatural for people to desire a growing relationship with God if they don't have a relationship with God's people. And it's almost impossible to get people to follow a distant leader.

4. Prayer was foundational for me individually and for the church as a whole. As we prayed "change me" prayers, ministry began to happen. For the first time in my life, fasting and prayer became a way of life and others joined me. The prayer foundation laid in the early days was essential for everything that followed. This emphasis on prayer was observed by people as they visited the church. Eight years ago, I asked my then future wife to scrutinize the ministry areas of our church. She was involved in ministry in another church and could give an objective evaluation about our ministries. She stated that her church was probably doing most things better than we were except in the area of the prayer ministry. Prayer was the fiber of our church. People united in prayer can accomplish much.

5. Willingness to quickly own up to a poor decision or a poorly timed decision proved to build trust. I have found it easy to call others to change, but much harder to change myself when it involved major differences in my life. Early in my ministry, the church planned to build a 400-seat sanctuary. The plans had been made, the drawings presented and approved. Initially, I was the primary proponent. Yet, after I had gotten everyone on board with me, I began to realize God wanted us to wait. I struggled as a young leader with the decision of appearing foolish to the church and losing their respect as a leader, but I still felt we needed to put the plans on hold. A short time after we put the plans on hold, the church had an opportunity to purchase adjacent land that has enabled us to expand the ministries of the church. Had I not been willing to take the risk of appearing foolish, we would have been in a financial position that

would not have allowed us to purchase the land. This sort of transparency, sharing freely my areas of growth and weakness, has built loyalty and a genuine desire for personal growth in the leadership teams. It has never reduced respect for me or my leadership.

We began to look at experiences and opportunities which conveyed flexibility and an opportunity to go back if a decision didn't appear to be in the right direction. Readiness to say a decision lacked progress in the right direction enabled people to continue to look at new opportunities without the fear of being stuck with a bad outcome.

Leaders sometimes find it difficult to make changes they have not initiated. I am reminded of how difficult it is to change as I am challenged at home. I usually sit at the head of our table. On occasion, my son or daughter wants to change seats and sit in my chair. I sense a twinge of resistance to this insignificant request and feel uncomfortable. I have to remind myself that I too need to be willing to change so that I can continue to lead.

The pastor must provide inspiring, progressive, personal leadership. Confidence in God's specific call, joy in the particular appointment and place of service and inspiring, progressive, personal leadership of the pastor build an enduring and effective rural ministry.

1. Cultivate Strong Vision.

Vision is a deliberate choice to be God-centered, positive, and forward. It's an eagerness to invest in the future. It is building on strengths instead of being consumed with our weaknesses. A clear vision communicated often breeds excitement because every reasonably healthy person desires to be part of something bigger than themselves.

A businessman visited the church and read our visionary mission statement printed on the worship folder. He whispered to his wife during the service, "This is our church." He told me later this was the first time he had been in a church where "they knew where they were going." Robert Schuller says, "If you want to know how long a pastor plans on staying, ask him or her the dream. If the dream takes a year, that's how long he or she plans to stay. If it takes 10 years, or a lifetime, that's how long the person intends to stay."[1] A large, strong vision communicates both excitement and stability.

2. Deliberately Build Morale.

Lyle Schaller says low morale is the number one problem of the average church, rural or urban. People have an inherently low view of themselves and God. A wise pastor will help the church have a win or two pretty quickly and publicly celebrate every victory. Every time the congregation feels the thrill and excitement of God actually helping them step forward in a new area, morale will get stronger.

3. Consistently, Sincerely Affirm the Congregation.

The common perception is that rural people are backwards and non-progressive. We have farms in our community that have some of the finest technology in North America. Consumers come from all over the United States to purchase cabinets and furniture from our skilled craftsmen. Frontline thinkers in the business communities around us make their homes in our community. They rarely get the opportunity to use their expertise and technological skills outside of their place of employment. We acknowledge their gifts and abilities and regularly affirm our need and appreciation for them in the life of the church.

4. Build a Good Name in the Community

Respect for the church and its leadership must be strong, especially in a rural community. Often in a small town, growth is suspect and sheep-stealing is a common charge. I made attendance at the ministerial meetings a priority and participated in as many community events as possible. I shared with the pastors in the ministerial association that because of our great concern for those who were lost, we would be aggressively contacting the community. We would target only those who were not attending church and encourage anyone who identified with a home church to be active in it and supportive of it.

Within those boundaries, promote aggressively. When a restaurant or store makes a management or inventory change, they spend money to advertise. They know it will more than pay back their investment. Your community needs to know it is not business as usual at your church.

5. Concentrate on the Strengths of Your Community.

A rural church typically has tremendous potential for growth. Each church and pastor will have to scout out their area for what potential is best for them to mine. Robert Schuller's urging, "Find a need and fill it," is the best approach for the rural church. In every community there are unmet needs and the church body that plans to meet those needs is the one that will grow. Companies are moving to our area because of the strong work ethic. People are coming to Sugarcreek to work because the work demand exceeds the work force. Walking alone at night is safe. A 1998 poll says 41% of Americans would like to live in a rural area within 10 years.[2] I continually remind myself I am in a terrific place and I tell my people the same thing. Our church is a little distance for some people, but they have decided, "A church alive is worth the drive."

6. Highlight Ministries Regularly and Make Heroes of the Ministers Leading Them.

The people of your church are the reason good things happen. Highlight that and be the head cheerleader for the ministries they begin and continue. Letting your people succeed at fulfilling their dreams within the mission of the church will cause them to thrive individually and corporately. One man told me, "You are the first pastor we have had who let us spread our wings."

7. Plan Your People Investments Well.

The pastor needs to be a friend to everyone, but prime time must be spent equipping the ones who will multiply the ministry. Following the example of Jesus, I worked with the crowd, but spent priority time with the handful I could see would make the critical difference in multiplying the ministry. My superintendent called me to task over this and told me to do a better job of "spreading the attention around." I shared with him that the strategy of Jesus was to find a few potential leaders, develop them and build a vision in them. I took people on visitation with me. I let them learn the ropes with me—try, fail, and keep on until they found their niche and developed confidence. I let them know it is all right to say "no" to areas that are not their calling, to try something new, and back out when you discover it is not a fit.

Satisfaction and fulfillment need to be the rule, not the exception in ministry positions. Whatever you sow, you will reap. Sow gratitude as your people minister. I make literally hundreds of "thank-you" phone calls and write hundreds of personal notes. One lady, now a loyal member, said it was the first tangible appreciation she had received in 35 years of ministry. Spend money on your leaders. Send them to workshops. For years now, we have given our leaders scholarships to the best leadership development seminars and helped them participate in as many training workshops as possible. It creates a sense of worth and destiny. Take groups of workers to other successful churches to see what they are doing right and what you can learn from them. A group of 10-12 men meet with me monthly, and we discuss the 8-10 books we have read during that time. The church that outgrows its leaders is a church certain to decline and die.

8. Emphasize Excellence within Your Capabilities.

Limit music ministry and do the songs well, rather than do something new and different that you can't pull off with excellence. I said to our soloists, "I would rather you sing a simple hymn with confidence and excellence, than struggle through a contemporary song." We started acting like an excellent, effective ministry. When I go on vacation, I make certain that the guest speaker is as capable or better than I. We began working on our building to make it as attractive and functional as any in the city. Our people developed such a love and appreciation for serving with excellence that our new facility has restrooms in all the children's rooms, a 20x20 foot reverse image screen in the sanctuary, and is professionally decorated.

Commit to regularly and consistently pay the price. Everything has a price tag and the price tag of successful ministry is high. Bobby Knight denied the common knowledge that successful teams are set apart by the desire to win. "Nonsense," he said. "Every team has the desire to win. What sets the champions apart is the desire to prepare."[3]

9. Plan Big Days.

Friends' Day, Fill a Pew Day, Children's Day—all these have worked very well for us. One day we filled the church with helium balloons and let them go after the service. Special days break the routine, build anticipation, and stave off predictability.

Along with the Big Days, there must be consistent weekly ministry. The quality of the ministry must be as high as possible all the time. A few great days or even two great worship services a month will not make it; people want to depend on a well-prepared and presented opportunity for worship weekly. Consistency gives people the freedom to invite their family and friends to worship because they know there is quality ministry happening and they will not be embarrassed by what takes place. Adult ministry cannot be strong when children's or youth ministry is weak and ineffective. The high quality of ministry across the church must be fairly consistent.

10. Get Organized.

The rural church has often deserved the reputation as a congregation that doesn't know which end is up. I know of situations where business was conducted during the worship service and the pastor joked about singing a few extra songs and "letting God speak to us because I'm not very well prepared this morning." We are consistently commended on the organization and planning evident in our ministry. Our efforts have reaped many benefits. I would attend SFMC myself, whether it was in the country or the heart of a beautiful city, because I am doing all I can to pastor a church that would please me if I was church hunting.

11. Let Leaders Lead.

A pastor must be secure enough to release ministry to capable lay leaders. A couple of years ago, a lady in our church came to me with a vision for developing a Mother of Preschoolers (MOPS) ministry. I saw that she had leadership gifts and had a real vision for what she saw was needed and so my response to her was, "Go for it." Today, MOPS is one of the largest outreach ministries of our church. My responsibility in this was to be an encourager to her, to pray for her, to let her know I was there for her if she had questions, and then to get out of the way and let her lead. A well-known fact in Sugarcreek is that a quick way to "make Dwight uncomfortable is to call him Reverend Mason." I stress frequently that I hold the office of pastor, but all of us are ministers. Some have tremendous capabilities to lead and I am anxious to release them, telling them often that the most significant thing they will ever do in life will probably be through this church.

As they lead, involve as many as possible in new steps. We did numerous surveys about what people desired in ministry, what they felt would benefit the community. We published and promoted the results, allowing everyone to see what others were thinking and to confirm that the leadership was in tune with the congregation. We used our current groups and Sunday school classes to give birth to new groups and classes. They experienced the joy of partnership in progress.

12. Making Disciples Is Our Primary Responsibility

To fulfill what Christ commanded, all of our programs and activities are evaluated on their contribution to the winning, building and equipping of disciples. Some time ago, a man visited our church and rushed up to me after our service, wanting to know "what had happened to Mr. So and So." I wasn't sure what he meant and so I continued to question him. His response to me was that he had come to the church for one reason and that was to find out what was making a difference in the life of his acquaintance. He explained to me that the gentleman's life was now so different that he had to come and see what was making that difference.

13. Focus Outward.

Encourage stewardship at every level and lead the church with your own giving. Missions giving will grow your church. One of our best experiences was building a church in Africa while we built our own new building. In our last fund-raising event, which raised over $1,000,000 for our newest addition, we agreed to tithe our income to financially support one of our missionary families.

14. Be Willing to Lose a Little to Win Big.

No one likes to be with someone who always has to win. Choose your battles wisely. During a promotional time at the church, I had placed a large banner across the front of the platform area that went along with our theme. A lady told me that she didn't like the banner there because she couldn't see the cross. I moved the banner. Even though to me it seemed to be an insignificant thing, moving the banner helped her feel that she mattered and that her pastor didn't have to always be the winner.

To determine what must be lost in order to win big, regular evaluation is essential. The proverb "practice makes perfect" is only partially true. If I practice something that is wrong, it will never become perfect. Only evaluated practice makes a positive difference. An unevaluated church will decline.

15. Continually Look Forward.

Celebrate from where you have come, but always keep the picture of the preferred future in front of you and your people. This can take the form of prayer requests, asking God for the people, equipment, and wisdom to reach the growing ministry needs. Continuous growth and improvement will characterize your way of "doing church."

Proverbs 20:5 says, "The purposes of a man's heart are deep waters, but a man of understanding draws them out." Change may or may not come as quickly in the rural area, but a good leader will understand his people and lead with that understanding. Our world has gotten smaller through transportation, communication and technology. The city is just minutes away and people expect the same quality in church that they see in the city and in their work places. I constantly remind myself that I usually don't accomplish as much in a year as I would like, but God has enabled us to accomplish more in the last five years than was ever dreamed or imagined. The vision God gave me when I came will not be accomplished in a short period of time. What does it matter if the vision takes five or ten or more years? In the end, I want to look back and have a sense that I have been faithful to God's call for my life and that I have enjoyed the journey.

ENDNOTES

[1]Robert Schuller, *Your Church Has Real Possibilities* (Glendale: Regal, 1974), pp. 45-46.
[2]Paul R. Ausherman, "Country Churches—More Than History," *Net Results,* Aug. 1997: p. 10.

Chapter 11

Menu Ministry

Preparing a Table Before Them

by Joe Seaborn

*T*housands of churches across America know they are not the growing, vibrant, faith communities they want to be. At the same time, they fear the sort of changes which the consultants and innovative prophets recommend. What do we do? Do we settle for prolonged terminal illness leading to death? Do we risk the drastic therapies which, if they don't kill you, make you sick in the process?

There is an alternative to many churches which seek to revitalize their ministries. The faith and traditions of our forefathers and the stewardship of preceding generations need not be wasted. Perhaps the best method for transitioning traditional churches is to add new ministries designed to reach new people, while not deleting from the ongoing ministries and styles loved and appreciated by many.

The genius behind this seemingly simple strategy is that people do not so much fear the new things as they fear losing the old things. By primarily adding to and not taking from an existing ministry offering, you can avoid a lot of the negative energy which fear induces. There are prices to be paid for this sort of strategy, but they are often much better than alternative, prolonged impotency and eventual church death. This kind of approach is more like a bypass than a transplant. The potential within many of our churches lies in the courage to pursue this sort of ministry transition.

Dr. Joe Seaborn is a great model for leading a menu ministry in a midwestern town in a conservative part of the country, where innovative ideas are often suspect. Joe earned a Harvard doctorate, is the author of seven books and numerous articles. He is the president of Guidelines for Living, a weekly television broadcast which deals with practical issues in daily living. He is married to Dr. Mary Seaborn and is father to Mary Joy, Joseph, and Jerolyn. Under his leadership, College Wesleyan Church in Marion, Indiana, has nearly doubled and increased the diversity of people being reached.

I can point to the spot where it happened. For two months I had known I would be assuming the senior pastoral position of a university church. Depending on your point of view, it was either a church rich in tradition or steeped in inertia. Pride oozed out of the nameplates on the ends of the pews. Brass plaques blossomed alongside the flowers. You could feel the inertia circulating in the hallways.

I have lived long enough to know that you should never tear down a fence until you know why it was put up. So I gave myself to the task of discovering a way to preserve and proceed at the same time. How could we hold on and turn loose with the same hands? How could we praise the plaques and still move the pews?

For two months I sat in the far back corner of that church, knowing that in a few days I would be up front. But what to do? I watched one group grimace when we sang a chorus and another group clam up when we turned to a hymn. I watched people check off components in the order of worship like it was a "To Do" list. I saw capable Christians wasting their gifts. I searched my spirit and scouted my mind, and still for days I remained firmly planted in midair.

I can still show you the spot where I found an answer. I was standing midway down aisle 11 in the local supermarket; the cereal aisle. As a boy, I had stocked grocery store shelves and remembered opening cases of cornflakes and Cheerios and Shredded Wheat. That was about it. There must have been a few more varieties in Grand Rapids, but the "mom and pop" establishment where I spent my boyhood didn't stock them. My mother rotated among those three kinds. (I still hate Cheerios!)

But now in this supermarket, sprawled out in front of me north to south, flowed a sea of cereal. I took time to count. One shopper even thought I was the inventory boy. When I finally ran out of breath, I had counted one hundred and thirty-four different kinds of cereal. I'll spare you the list, but not the insight. This breakthrough morphed two months worth of nebulous thoughts into a cogent whole.

I would lead that church by providing more choices. There would be a distinct place for hymns in one service and a place for choruses in another, a host of special groups and a call to remain one body. We would plant churches without ever building a new facility. We would offer more options for ministry and outreach than this church had ever dreamed of before. Instead of folding an aging women's ministry to start a new one, we would keep them both. We would parallel traditional programs with creative new programs. There would be layers of ministry within a single range of need. Instead of asking everybody to accept one style, we would respond to their preferences by adding one service with Mozart and another with Michael W. We would offer a menu of ministries.

Two years have passed since the grocery aisle epiphany. Lots of ideas have flopped. Lots have flown. The great church which hired me is becoming even greater. Every week the sense of excitement flows over the fellowship like a warm front moving in. And we've only just begun.

When visitors ask our people why the church is coming along so well, the answers make a menu of teachings all their own. Let me get the lay people up here for you to hear.

(1) *"We're trying new things and people are enjoying the freshness."*
—Brenda

There are two deadly "P's" which plague the church. They are pacing and predictability. Pacing has to do with the starts, the stops, the flow and the "slow" of the worship. If you want to get a sense of the pacing of your worship, videotape it. If you're like us, you'll sit and groan at all the dull dead spots when all you see is somebody looking at somebody else to see if it's time for something else to happen.

The other killer is predictability. If people can all but guess what's coming next in the worship, worship is weakened. The next step is for people to make a joke of it. Congregational lampoon. Mock it. "Different text, same sermon." Then a light laugh. But they won't do that if you keep them a little off balance. You'll remember that the Pharisees were sure that Jesus would walk on their red carpet. When He showed up at the seaside with a grasshopper-eating prophet wrapped in a gunny sack, they rolled up their carpet pretty quickly. If Jesus was anything, He was

149

unpredictable. Ask the woman at the well. Ask Zacchaeus. Jesus invited Himself to Zacchaeus' house. I doubt that short saint ever got over it.

Freshness doesn't require large numbers. It does require forethought. You'll never be fresh if you're preparing the worship as it flies. But take reading the Bible. Instead of reading the passage from the pulpit, menu your approach. Have a layman read it, or read it while standing in the center aisle as a symbol of the fact that the Word belongs among the people. Or have your sound man read it without being seen by the congregation. This will remind them that it is a Word from a Source beyond the room. Or let a group of people gather on the platform and read it in unison. Or let children stumble through it and you'll get a happy hearing. If you REALLY want it to be heard, stick your lips on the microphone and whisper it. People will fall out of their pews to hear a whisper! If I really want something to be heard, I always whisper it. It's always the most remembered sentence in the sermon.

What you're fighting is predictability. One of the senior adults in our fellowship put it this way, "I can hardly wait to get to church. You just never know how they're going to tell the old, old story in a new, new way." Let me challenge you to do it. Add one component to your worship this coming Sunday which nobody could predict. Listen to the comments afterward and see if it doesn't get in your blood.

And one is probably enough. You don't want variation to become the theme. The unchanging gospel is still your focus.

(2) *"Things are always changing, but the regular programs keep going too."* —Steve

I tell my people often, "Never push the envelope. Open another one." One gospel would do. But Christ gave us four. Go figure. We are always thinking "bi-level" or "tri-level" around here. If a person's schedule won't allow him to join a LifeNet group (our name for the menu of specialty groups such as GolfLinks or GriefCare), we urge them to start one of their own. If one group wants denominational curriculum and another wants to study the Bible directly, no problem. There's room at the Cross for both. By offering the old patterns and continually carving new ones, we generate both a spirit of relief that "we still have our church" and a sense of joy that "the church is changing like crazy."

For example, look at the worship services. At this point, we have four with another one on the drawing boards. Each of the four services is unique, down to the sermon. Nothing is repeated. If people hear the message in one service, they are the first and only ones to hear it. The message is not developed generically, but with a specific congregation in mind.

This mammoth process is possible because we involve lay people. As pastor, I establish the themes for each service as the Lord guides me. Then I place that sacred trust of truth in the hands of lay people who help to develop the flow of the service. That leaves me time to focus on the preaching of the Word. They treat the privilege with astounding care and sensitivity. They suggest songs or hymns, recommend a skit idea (which the SkitCrew develops), draw a great reading from church history, recommend a brief testimony from someone they know or give any number of other suggestions that make for richness and depth. By Thursday, I have their recommendations back in hand and can give them the final shaping before I stand to guide the whole on Sunday morning.

Let me give you a feel for the four services. When people are called on to participate in one of the services, they receive these guidelines to help them sense the mood we are seeking to capture for that particular hour.

(a) **FAMILY:** In this service we are looking for music that fits with a contemporary, populist style. This is not the place for fugues and Mozart. The Second Chapter of Acts and Carman are the right feel here. There needs to be gentle, vibrant feel to the song. A little up-tempo would do just fine. Here's a quick set of words to describe the spirit of the worship: pleasant, warm, friendly, earthy, gentle, like a quick swirl of vanilla layered on a sugar cone.

(b) **CELEBRATION:** This is our "X-ers" worship. It is deliberately geared to a generation for whom the praise band and worship choruses will be second nature for the rest of their lives. It has drama and a ring of sterling authenticity. The music for this service will stay in the contemporary mainstream.

As you plan to participate in this worship, include music that reflects these characteristics: upbeat, contemporary, lilting, worshipful, relational, warm.

(c) **CATHEDRAL:** This is our more formal worship hour. The means of grace, the great worship components which have endured across the centuries of the church, and the more liturgical elements figure into this style. The music will be hymnic, but not stiff or stodgy.

As you prepare for involvement in this service, you will want to offer a musical selection that is marked by these features: warm, dignified, lofty, rich with meaning, worshipful, stately, restrained.

(d) **FESTIVAL:** This service is designed to be a free, energetic hour of spontaneous celebration and out-loud praise. As you choose your song to share in this worship, please keep the following tones in mind: upbeat, festive, cadenced, life-related, engaging, intense and intimate. You will probably not be able to find any Christian music that is too free and vigorous for this congregation.

Interested in knowing what we plan for the fifth style? It'll be GOSPEL. We have this bunch who think that all the other groups will be nothing but warm-up for the Cathedrals when we get to heaven. OK, OK, enough already. Can anybody read shape notes?

(3) *"People are involved. They have both ownership and leadership."*
    —Julia

The value of that is as obvious as the nose on an airplane. People who participate care. People who serve, grow. People who have a personal ministry build the corporate ministry. We come up with "every way under the Son" to get peoples' hands on a slice of the Kingdom. The little jobs include the teens carrying my Bible to the pulpit on Sunday morning. A second set of ushers open doors in the parking lot. Couriers run errands for the indoor ushers. Laymen do skits on the sermon theme. Senior adults write short poems on assignment for inclusion in the bulletin. You name it and we try to find somebody to do it.

Last Sunday, I handed out a list of 65 new ministries we wanted somebody around here to start doing. If you want a copy of "Menu 65," drop a note and we'll have a "Minister of Mailings"!

(4) *"They do all the basics here, but they do them with lots of creativity."*
    —Katie

Back to the menu. You need the meat and potatoes. No church worth its salt can live on salt. You've got to have a regular biblical intake at the center of it all. Take preaching. I keep it front and center. But I make it my first point to menu the way I present the points. Over a series of Sundays, I will use ellipsis, alliteration, an unfolding sentence, story telling, in-the-sermon skits, key passage phrases and occasionally a testimonial. Sometimes I stay by my notes, sometimes I stray from my notes and sometimes I gray trying to read my notes. Our pulpit is an understudy for the Rock of Gibraltar so sometimes I'm behind it, sometimes I'm beside it and sometimes—so they can see me—I remove it.

Just to make sure the people know that I am about the basics, in the Sunday evening service I am currently preaching my way through the entire Bible. It's a sermon series that will take seven years.

(5) *"There's a ton of attention to the personal touch."* —Bob

People worship best where people matter first. If you will first sit where they sit, a-la-Ezekiel, they will walk where God guides. If an order of worship keeps us from seeing a pained spirit in need of immediate prayer, we have missed the gate and hit the fence. Somebody said about Sam Jones, "He always saw the faces beyond the deadly statistics."

Here are three ways to keep the personal touch high, no matter the size of your church. Our hi-tech world needs a hi-touch love.

(a) *Layered Letters.* Write two, three, four or more-way letters. I write letters to two or more people and talk to them as if they were all sitting in a circle around me. It warms them to each other and sets up a "wow" of a friendship when they actually do meet.

(b) *Living Roses.* Every few Sundays, we buy a half-dozen red roses and surprise a few folks. Right in the middle of the worship, we grab the handheld mike and head into the congregation. There sits Clara Goodman, saint in residence, mother in Israel, hand of God. When I place that rose in her hands and a hug around her neck, the moment glows with power. You raise what you praise. Over there sits Christin, youth in a tough world, prematurely mature, Christ's ambassador to the local high school. The rose matches her dress so I thank her for being ready. The people laugh and cry and grow.

Guess what people enjoy most about the rose moments? Who'll get them? The element of surprise. The unpredictable. Who will it be this Sunday? What will he say about them? Talk about a return on a ten dollar investment!

(c) *"Bisits."* Leave the office and do "bisits." (rhymes with visits) A "bisit" is a "visit with a busy person." If people visit our church, we have a policy that rhymes, "KNOCK ON THE DOOR WITHIN TWENTY FOUR." We don't go in—unless God seems to urge it. We stand on the step and say something like this, "I wanted to stand here on your step and tell you how thrilled we were to have you and your family with us yesterday. I hope so much you can do it again. That's all I really wanted to say. I know how busy life is, but I wanted to make sure you knew that from the bottom of our heart, we really thank you for coming." Zoom. Out of there. We drive twenty miles, spent thirty seconds on the threshold, and we're gone. When we drive away you can still see their jaw laying on the step! You can almost read their minds, "Did that man drive this whole distance just to tell me that? Twenty miles to tell me thanks!" Yep. That's visitation for the twenty-first century. Remember, in our hi-tech world, hi-touch is the key. You wait, it'll be a hit.

Ideally we "bisit" when it's raining or snowing. That lets people know even more, just how serious we are about it. We sure want them to come to church if it's raining or snowing, so we figure we need to model. Thirty seconds is enough. It shows you care, but it respects their time. "Bisits" have been the single greatest reason why visitors give us a second chance to love them. If you have your highlighter handy, this is the paragraph to paint.

(6) *"We are learning how to celebrate and affirm the uniqueness of each generation."* —Jonathan

Iconoclasts never create movements, they only destroy monuments. Fighting the past has never energized the present. Ralph Nader is no world changer. Billy Graham is the world changer. And he has a personal policy of never answering a critic. People who change the world don't gripe about it; they grip it. Both hands. In love. They seize and squeeze until somebody knows they mean eternal business.

We mix up the ages on the platform. We have inter-generational services. We have senior citizens adopt seniors in school. Call it "Senior Hi." The front of our church directory explodes with pictures that hit every age and stage of our congregation. It's a point we mean to make.

(7) *"We have things going on for almost every known need in the church. People can find all kinds of places to connect."* —Ted

A few Sundays back, as I was walking down the hall toward the sanctuary, a key leader in the church tugged my coat sleeve. "Pastor, do you think we could ever consider starting a small group for single parents?" "Sure," I said, "Let's do it next Sunday." He thought I was kidding. "No, pastor, it's a real need." "Well, if it's real, let's not wait. Let's see what we can do right away."

Sometimes as a leader I throw myself off the cliff and look for a set of wings on the way down. I called the Sunday school superintendent and set the idea in motion. The following Sunday a young lady who knew how to love and listen was standing in front of five single parents. When I asked Pat how the class was going, she grinned, "Trying to stay ahead of them is like laying track in front of an oncoming train." Talk about a learning curve!

Create new classes, new groups, new friendships, new patterns. When you go to the produce department, you may only buy bananas, but you can't help but enjoy standing there with mounds of fruits and vegetables laid out like an amphitheater around you. When you pick up a bunch of bananas, you feel like you're getting the whole market. That's what involvement does in a church. Nobody can do it all, but everybody can feel the whole.

If you have a big ego that needs to soak up all the glory, you'll want to avoid a menu approach to ministry. You've heard the line, "Every person has a favorite pastor." When you diversify ministry, you can go ahead and assume that for many people, their favorite "pastor" will be the person who is giving them the primary personal attention and care. For a lot of the people who sit in our services, I'm the third or fourth-string pastor. In some cases, they still don't know me. I love it—sorta. But if somebody else can reach out and link people with God through this fellowship, it leaves me free to knock on another door and love still another person to Jesus.

(8) *"Our pastor is sensitive to people and has found several ways to lead them to Christ."* —Ruth

Evangelism is still the heartbeat of the body. New models are emerging here too. We have tried any number of approaches, including the time-honored altar call and hymn of invitation at the end of the worship. Our two most successful evangelism methods have been a surprise. One of them involves a group. In the worship hour and also in the bulletin, we announce a special meeting which will focus on the gospel message and how to receive Christ as Savior and Lord. People actually come. They come with the express purpose of praying to receive Christ. I've called it for Saturday morning, but other times might work just as well.

The other method that has had amazing success is the "Invitation to Lunch." It really ought to be called the "Invitation at Lunch." We do lunch, but I offer the more lasting invitation too. I urge people who want to be saved to call and invite me to lunch. I promise that we will talk over lunch, then go to their car and close our time with a prayer for salvation. This approach requires high initiative on their part. They have to call, knowing full well what the lunch will mean. I'm happy for the free meal, but I am even happier for the manna from heaven on which the fortunate person can feed forever.

Christianity can be—must be—culturally current. Christ is our eternal contemporary. In our time, becoming all things to all people means at the very least that we provide our choice-conscious culture with choices at church.

Before you go, let me hand you three words one more time. Keep them handy. See if they can help you take your group to a new level of life and love. Here they are: MENU, UNPREDICTABLE, "BISIT."

155

Thanks for receiving them. They're a gift. A trio of treasures we have found to give away.

The very culture in which we live and move and have our being is brimming with variations and choices. Forty-five RPM records had two songs, CDs have twelve. Solitary stores have moved to the mall. Restaurants market the number of items on the buffet. Baskin-Robins has surrounded chocolate and vanilla with a flood of other flavors. Heinz is way past 57. I probably need to do a recount on Aisle Number 11. And I will, as soon as I glance in this classroom to see how Pat's doing on her railroad!

Chapter 12

Transforming a Traditional Church

by Bob Huffaker

*I*n southern California where we lived for years, we spent days off tooling around Newport Beach and the Balboa Bay Peninsula. We typically drove across the bridge to get there and took the ferry to get back. The boys loved the process of driving onto the small barge, getting out of the car, and "driving" on the water. Transitioning a church is a lot like building a bridge, connecting to different styles, cultures, paradigms and linking them under the umbrella of a single ministry. To transform a traditional church into one which reaches a different subculture is more like using a ferry. The goal is to get from one side to the other, without the solid link. Some congregations and leaders are more interested in dramatically changing the corporate cultures of their churches because they are no longer growing or reaching the people around their community. Sometimes they just sense that God is calling them to do something significantly different. The stories abound of such churches doing the crash *and burn thing—leaving hard feelings, a devastated pastor, and smoldering embers which prevent successors from starting another fire in the same area.*

But just because a few take a nose dive should not thwart us from considering the possibilities of such dramatic church change. The key is whether or not it is God's will and whether or not the leader has the ability to do it without killing the congregation. Bob Huffaker is one of those uniquely suited to achieving dramatic transformation without wreaking havoc. Grove City Church of the Nazarene has grown significantly under Bob's leadership since 1989, from 600 to over 2000. Now in the process of building a $7,000,000, 3200 seat auditorium on 63 acres, the church is listed in Elmer Towns' book, 10 Sunday Schools That Dared To Change. *The church has become a vibrant outreach center in Ohio and for a few years has been the fastest growing Church of the Nazarene in the United States. Bob is married to Libby and has four children.*

The church that is not willing to change is willing to die! If you keep doing the same things you have always done, you will keep getting the same results you have always gotten!

- Why is it that over 85% of all Protestant churches are plateaued or in decline?
- Why is it so difficult to make the kind of changes necessary in this accelerated culture?
- What kind of church will it take to reach our kind of world?
- Could it be that making change is too costly?
- Could it be that leaders are too fearful?
- Could it be that it takes too much effort?
- Could it be that many leaders just do not know how to make the transition from the past into the present?

How Do You Transition a Traditional Church?

Our church has made significant changes in the last eight years. What is transition? What is traditional? The dictionary defines "transition" as the state of passing from one place to another, or change. "Traditional" refers to the customs that are being continued. These are simplistic definitions, but change, whether it be in the church or the world, causes us to venture into areas of insecurity, territorialism, and turf ownership. Following are my ideas of what has caused the significant growth in our spirit as well as the complementary numerical increase.

Transition in any church has to begin in the heart of the pastor. There must be a conviction, a passion, and an understanding of the necessity of change. Then the pastor must ask himself, "Am I willing to take the risk?"

With change comes conflict, stress, and sometimes even pain. Creating positive change is one of the most difficult tasks a leader faces. A tremendous amount of energy must be exerted to bring about positive change.

There is a right and a wrong way to create change. When change is unsuccessful, it is usually not because the project is unworthy, but because the person trying to create the change doesn't know how to do it effectively. Most negative results are not because of the change itself, but because the process of changing was not correct.

How "We" Changed . . .

We came to Grove City Church of the Nazarene in 1989. It was a good, healthy, but traditional church, which had just relocated and built a multipurpose building on a 27-acre tract of land across from the high school. The church had just celebrated its twenty-fifth anniversary and was running about 600 in morning worship attendance.

We had come from a church in a small, west Texas town that had gone through some major changes and experienced good growth. In thirteen years, it had grown from 60 to 500. The majority of the growth was due to the relocation of the building, a new sanctuary, and the change of worship style. We moved from a traditional worship style to a contemporary style.

Upon our arrival in Grove City, I immediately felt God had brought us here to lead this church into a lifestyle of worship. Perhaps a better word would be a participatory style of worship.

Over the past several years, I had been convicted of how little our people participated in the worship. We had made good spectators out of them, but very few really entered into worship in a participatory way. I wondered how the church had lost its celebratory, free spirit in worship. I had heard how the old-time Nazarenes would sing, shout, clap, and praise God until the glory came down! But I guess we had become so fearful that people would call us charismatic that we began to change to a more subdued, refined, dignified worship style in order not to be identified with the Pentecostal crowd.

I was convinced in my spirit that if the Bible was true when it said that "God inhabits the praises of His people," He did not have much of a dwelling place in the people called Nazarenes, for there was very little praise in our service. Second Corinthians 3:17 says: *"Where the Spirit of the Lord is, there is freedom."* Once again, I was not seeing much freedom in our worship services. Was the Spirit of the Lord absent because of the lack of praise in our worship?

Out of these convictions came a passion in my spirit to teach and lead our people in praise and worship—unashamed—because when *"He is lifted up, He will draw all men to Him"* (John 12:32 paraphrase).

Almost immediately as we began the "new" worship style (actually, it began back in the book of Acts), the church began to experience accelerated growth.

What Steps Did We Take?

Step One: Change of Attitude

I began to preach and teach on attitude, because I knew if the church was going to make major changes, the peoples' attitudes would have to be right. The success of any major change is determined before the change is ever made. It all hinges on attitude. If you think you can or if you think you can't—you are right!

Were we going to "have the mind of Christ" in our change to becoming the kind of church that could reach our kind of world? Everything rises and falls on attitude. If the people were going to be negative toward me and the changes I felt God wanted us to make, I knew it would be an impossible task.

Step Two: Educate! Educate! Educate!

I knew all the staff had to be "on the same page." They had to understand and believe in what I was trying to do in regard to becoming a "contemporary" church. I began to educate my staff.

I educated the leadership on the biblical principles of praise and worship. For example, I began teaching the Hebrew names for God. How can you hallow His name if you don't know His name? I also did a series of messages on the "Seven Principles of Praise." All of this teaching was to give a better understanding of what it meant for God's people to praise Him. This teaching began to bring about a new freedom and joy in our worship services. Basically, I gave our people permission to praise God in our worship services!

Step Three: Cast the Vision

I began to cast the vision of where I felt God wanted to lead us. I began to define the purpose for the Grove City Church of the Nazarene. I wanted to elevate their vision and not just by reaching the denominational quotas.

I have always felt our denomination does not challenge its pastors and churches in a big enough way. I understand it is very difficult to find a "one size fits all shoe," and I understand how hard it is to move away from what has worked in the past. But somehow I knew had to lift our vision. I began to talk about reaching our city for God and how we were going to do it by reaching young families, ministering to their children, and becoming a church that is relevant, with a worship style that is appealing.

Step Four: Focus on the Outward

As we moved into a different style of worship, I knew there would be some people, especially older people, who would not enjoy the "new songs," the new band, the praise team, and the louder music. They would miss their "old favorites."

I also knew the self is not always crucified in the sanctified, that self would begin to rise up and say, "We liked it better the old way. Let's get rid of the drums . . . let's bring back the hymn books . . . let's stop singing all those choruses.

I began to meet with my senior citizen group and explain to them why we were doing what we were doing. I encouraged them to focus on the outward, rather than the inward. I challenged them to allow the church to use the kind of music that would reach the young, unchurched families, rather than sing just the songs they enjoyed. Once they understood why I was doing what I was doing, the complaining began to cease.

Step Five: Build Rapport

I knew I had to have the support of my influencers, so I put forth extra effort to build a positive rapport with the lay leaders in the church. I spent extra time sharing my dreams and goals, asking for their input and advice, but never losing sight of my goals.

I also knew I needed people to run interference for me. I sought an elderly gentleman who had influence with the senior citizens in the church. I knew he probably would be the first to hear about their negative feelings toward the changes. He was able to take tremendous pressure off me.

I made sure I built rapport with the people. I did not avoid them just because some of them were negative toward the changes. I always made a point to drop in on their meetings and potluck dinners. I made sure they knew I loved them. Many pastors make the mistake of avoiding the people who disagree with them.

Step Six: Establish Credibility

I always tried to keep the changes in a positive light. I would brag publicly and from the pulpit about the people's ability to accept change, always showing the benefits and the results of the positive changes that had taken place. Quite often I would talk about us being the church on the cutting-edge, the church that was leading instead of following. I tried to assure them that we had a reverse gear—that if something did not work after a time of trial, we would do something different.

I wanted them to know that the changes being made were not for my personal preference, but were for the good of the church and the Kingdom of God. I wanted them to know this was not just another preacher's whim, but a conviction, and that I was there to build the Kingdom of God through the church. I did my best to establish credibility, never promising more than I would produce, always being aboveboard with my plans and decisions.

Step Seven: Produce

Make sure you produce. Nothing succeeds like success. If the church is growing and increasing during the change process, it takes away the clout of the negative people. But if the church plateaus or declines, this is fodder for fuel that will make it much more difficult, if not impossible, to bring the necessary change. It is imperative that you show regular growth while you are making change.

Step Eight: Make Hard Decisions

Be willing to make hard decisions. Most pastors want everyone to like or to accept them. This is just human nature. They do not want to lose anyone from their church. Some pastors want to have unanimous approval of the entire church or at least that of the church board and staff. They find it impossible to make difficult decisions if the results will cause conflict. This is especially true in a smaller church.

Some people will never be willing to accept change in their church. I believe no church can grow until it is willing to risk losing some people. We had to release someone who had been at the keyboard for sixteen years because of philosophical differences and an inflexibility in adjusting to what we were trying to accomplish. This was a very difficult and risky decision. Without this change, it would have been impossible to make subsequent changes necessary to achieve our goals. We lost the member and his family to another church, where he was able to use his gifts in ministry.

You may like one flavor of ice cream and I may like another, but the bottom line is that we both like ice cream. That man is still serving God as he follows the road laid before him. Sometimes pastors must be willing to make hard decisions.

Step Nine: Establish Credibility

"People don't care how much you know until they know how much you care." "Walk your talk." "Do what you say." All of these phrases add up to credibility.

If you are a pastor, chances are that many pastors have preceded you. They may have had big dreams, big programs, big promises with big solutions, but either failed to follow through, dropped the ball or moved to another assignment. Why should the church have confidence in you when the last several pastors called for big changes and then left the congregation feeling betrayed and holding the bag?

Most churches like this would be skeptical of the new pastor. No wonder it is difficult to make change in these circumstances. No wonder they remind us, "We tried that before and it failed." The only solution is your credibility. If they see success in the present, their belief is added to your trustworthiness. If they see honesty, integrity, fairness, godliness, hard work, competency, vision, ability, confidence, courage, self-sacrifice, accomplishment, leadership, stamina, faith, humility, and a person of prayer and pure motives, then you are establishing credibility. It may sound superhuman, but it is not. Without credibility, you will never be able to instigate the change you desire.

Be real. Be genuine. And be aware that anything good in your life is not your doing, but is a gift from God. You can do nothing without Him.

Step Ten: Be Flexible

Every church is different. What works in Texas does not necessarily work in Ohio. What worked five or ten years ago probably will not work now. You will be dealing with different personalities and backgrounds. Everything is changing. As a result, be flexible. If you need to use the reverse gear, do it. You don't always have to be right. It's okay to say, "I'm sorry. I blew it. I made a mistake." Be willing to make some changes yourself. That's called flexibility.

You must be flexible enough to grow personally as the church grows numerically. Someone once said, "For every new level, there's a new devil." Stay knowledgeable about changing trends. Stay in contact with change agents, those innovative people or actions that can create change.

Stay current. Know what's current and working and go with winners. Always remember, "Methods are many and principles are few. Methods are always changing, but principles never do."

Conclusion

John Maxwell's Injoy tape, "Growth Equals Change," outlines ten steps a pastor must make in order to launch a new idea:

1. Let your enthusiasm for the new idea show.
2. Pre-sell to key people.
3. Explain all the reasons for changing.
4. Discuss the risks.
5. Show anticipated results.
6. Encourage the proper form of disagreement (the pros and cons of the new idea).
7. Promote what the project is, not what people think it is.
8. Establish short-range goals.
9. Keep influential people on board.
10. Stay on top of the problem. Be vigilant.[1]

There are other ways to change a traditional church, such as going to different worship styles at different times, having a sampling of services to target tastes of age groups, and even developing a blended service. Use whatever method will work best in your particular situation. There is one thing for certain: if you keep doing the same things you have always done, you will keep getting the same results you have always gotten.

Churches unwilling to change are willing to die. If we can make the transition from the old to the new, we will reap great benefits. We will have growing, healthy churches that are fulfilling God's purpose for their existence. The people who make up the changed church will experience a new joy, vision, and fulfillment as they reach out to their community to touch hundreds and thousands of lives.

ENDNOTES

[1]John Maxwell, "Growth Equals Change" (Injoy Ministries, 1989), audiocassette.

Chapter 13

Spare Some Change?

by Alan E. Nelson

*T*he final few chapters have to do with change. There are more similarities than differences when it comes to organizational changes within corporations and faith communities. We have much to learn from the growing mass of literature and research which is motivated by the need for change among the for-profit organizations. While our similarities are legion, our differences mean that as a general rule, churches are more reluctant to adopt change. One reason is that any change tends to be more significant since faith communities often provide more of a family culture than a typical business. When Sissy gets married and leaves home, the impact of the change outweighs an employee transition or new office software. Another reason that churches by their very nature tend to thwart change is the value of preserving ageless truths and theology, which are often confused with form and methods. The "keep change out" mind-set, although not theological, is very much a part of the typical church culture.

For most of my childhood, I grew up in churches which had experienced little change over the years, where consistency (good and bad) was the mode of operation. During my adult life, nearly all of the churches with which I've been associated have been congregations of *growth and health. As times change, so do the methods which produce prevailing congregations. As this book is being compiled, I am in the process of researching organizational change principles for a book project I'm working on with Gene Appel and Jim Mellado. Gene Appel came to what was a traditional congregation of 450 and has seen it change into a culturally relevant church of 4000-plus in Las Vegas. As president of the Willow Creek Association, Jim Mellado's eye for national and international trends provides a broad view of what is and is not happening among churches. Through this study, I was able to locate some of the primary factors which help organizations in general and churches in particular make effective transitions. Here is a very brief list of elements which make or break effective, significant change in a church.*

Churches of Change Are . . .

1. Leader Led: We stated it earlier, but it bears repeating. Managerial shepherds may be good at keeping the flock corralled and fed, but they are not wired to induce change. The primary purpose of a leader is to catalyze change within an organization. In congregations where there is no person gifted in leading in the senior/sole pastor role, don't count on a lot of positive change. I am not saying that only leaders pastor healthy churches. I am saying that congregations desirous of change need to find pastors who have leader gifts and skills. Although I am unaware of any studies done on the subject, I believe there is a very strong correlation between the small percentage of pastors who recognize their leadership gifts and the small percentage of congregations which are experiencing growth in recent years. You cannot stay the same in a changing environment and hope to grow.

But what if our church does not have a leader at the helm or what if I'm the pastor and I don't have strong leadership gifts? The bottom line is that a pastor need not be a leader to allow leadership to take place. In these situations, raising up strong, mature, lay leadership is key. Look for people in the church who are loyal, time-tested, and proven leaders in the marketplace. These are the people who must then be unleashed to provide vision and direction for the church seeking change, while the pastor disciples, nurtures, teaches, and affirms. The pastor must always be a part of the leadership process, but need not be the primary leader. Understanding how leadership works is a strong plus for those without natural or developed leading abilities. Some churches have staff members who are stronger leaders than the senior pastor. But putting staff in leadership roles is rarely a workable situation, due either to the senior pastor's insecurities, traditional views of proper chain-of-command, or the real or perceived misunderstanding of who is in charge.

2. Visionary Toward The Future: The words leader and vision are practically inseparable. Occasionally you'll find a leader without a vision, but usually only when there is burnout, complacency, or a need for healing. Without a vision, the people languish, wander and perish. A vision is a preferred future. When the future differs from the present, then a vision is needed. Many people confuse strategic plans and goals with visions. A vision comes first and transcends the other items. Vision has to do with the intangible, the felt, the big picture. Strategic plans and goals come next and have to deal with carrying out the vision. One of the most common and also intriguing confessions among ministry directors (lay or clergy) is, "My people just don't seem to want to change. I can't get anyone to enlist in this ministry. How can I lead when people are not on board?"

We've all been in that position, where leading seemed impossible because no one was willing to follow. What most people fail to understand is that a significant part of leading is helping people get the "want to." When people are already motivated and ready to buy into a dream, you only need half a leader. When the people are not yet aboard, you need a whole leader. The role of the leader is to cast a vision so that people want to change their priorities, buy into the new picture, and desire to get involved. Motivation comes after the vision, not the other way around. What you've admitted when you say that people are not interested in this project, is that you've not done your job as a leader. You have not cast a vision which makes this ministry or church so exciting that people desire to enlist. All sellers are not leaders, but all leaders must learn to sell effectively. As Napoleon said, "Leaders are dealers in hope." A vision is about hope, a preferred outcome, a better place to live, work, and worship. If you don't have an inner sense of where the church needs to be, then don't expect the people to know. Knowing the vision and then casting it effectively are the two primary pieces to the leadership jigsaw puzzle.

Imagine a large rubber band which you hold in your left hand. With your right hand, elevate one end of the rubber band while you continue to hold the other end in your left. The lower end represents where your church is now. The upper end represents the vision for the future. The difference is what must take place to obtain the preferred future. If the vision is too small, there is no tension and the people are not apt to be captivated. We all need this tension in our lives to keep us going, to wake us up for the next day, and to motivate us forward. Too much tension will snap the rubber band and is basically what happens when the vision is so lofty that no one is willing to get behind it. Keeping the right amount of tension in the process is a major responsibility of a leader.

3. Understanding the Psychology of Change: Organizations are basically extensions of people and therefore take on many of the characteristics of humans as well. Just as people in general are creatures of habit, organizations are designed to give us consistency, order, and help us avoid the overdose of constant change (chaos). Unfortunately, what they are designed to do works against the very nature of change. *Diffusion of Innovation*, a book by Everett Rogers, discusses the process by which people respond to new ideas and concepts.[1] Our culture is inundated with symbols and practices which reflect our reticence to implement change. For example, have you ever wondered why the typical computer keyboard is arranged as it is? Many of the most used letters are not in the areas most easily accessed by our most flexible fingers. The arrangement is certainly not alphabetical. The reason is that years ago, typists began being able to type faster than the machinery could respond. Jammed keys created problems, so typewriters were developed with key arrangements meant to slow typists. Years later, when the machines were improved to allow for faster typing, the letter arrangement had become so popular that people did not want to change. Now with lightning fast computer keyboards, we persist in using the same old key configuration, even though it was originally created to intentionally slow down typing. More effective key arrangements exist, but society has basically preferred to stick with the familiar.

Psychological testing reveals that a large majority of people do not change internally very well. Over 85% of people tend to avoid changes because they are stressful and contrary to their inner wiring. Therefore, to induce change in almost any organization means going against the tide of human nature. When you realize this, it is a miracle that any change takes place in organizations. Secular organizations and businesses have worked to counter this problem because the pain of being run out of business overrides going against human nature. A part of the church culture mind-set is to revere the past and retain the ageless truths of the Bible. Our "hold the fort" mentality with regard to doctrines and theology has drifted into the areas of methodology and form. Because we tend to identify our beliefs with more tangible things (the underlying problem with idolatry), we have confused our church culture with the more basic tenets of faith, worship, evangelism and discipleship. Understanding that most people are not wired for change should help the leader know why change is so challenging and why change needs intentional, concentrated effort.

4. Focused On Progressive Opinion Leaders: The good news is that although the majority of people in any given group are not predisposed to change, there exists a segment that is. Leaders who want to be effective in catalyzing change must seek to recognize and develop the group called progressive opinion leaders.

Of the 100% of people in your church, anywhere from 2-5% will be innovative. Innovators tend to like change for change's sake. They are the artists, entrepreneurs, and free thinkers. Innovators often come up with new ideas, but they often do not implement them, in part because they are perceived by the larger majority as loose cannons, mavericks, and organizationally dangerous.

The next 15% or so are progressive. They may not create the new ideas, but they are very open to change and do not fear it. They are quick to see the potential benefits of implementing new ideas as they are ready to see the dangers of status quo.

Following the progressives are the early adopters (25-35%). These people are not anti-change by nature, but neither are they ready to jump ship until they are convinced that there is an adequate or better ship ready to board. These people usually look to influencers among the progressives, who signal that they've checked the Promised Land and not only can we take the giants, but we can enjoy the benefits of the milk and honey.

The early adopters have counterparts in the late adopters (25-35%). These people are not apt to cross the Jordan until the progressives and early adopters have worn a well-marked path and proven that it is safe. When leaders hear the complaints of these people, they can sometimes get defensive or even take the offense by labeling them carnal and stubborn. Although they disguise it as criticism, sometimes it is just plain old fear that these late adopters are really confessing. Leaders need not overreact, but should communicate details, affirmation, benefits, and align themselves with their friends who are progressive and early adopters.

Finally, nearly every organization has a group which we might affectionately refer to as laggards (15%). These are the people who would question whether or not they should move, even if Jesus himself asked them. They are not necessarily anti-faith, but their strengths of consistency and commitment often become weaknesses of fear and entrenchment. These people are apt to cross only when they realize that staying where they are will require them to remain alone. Sometimes even that does not deter them, as many laggards are the ones who attend the final services before church doors are closed for good.

The most troublesome people in the life of a leader are the opinion leaders among the late adoptors and laggards. These vocal catalysts can create havoc for the one who would enter the Promised Land. They should not be overlooked or alienated, as is the first temptation of a naive leader. The key to effectiveness is not to battle the slow-to-change-naysayers as it is to positively motivate and develop the progressive opinion leaders.

Progressives tend to be characterized by a positive demeanor toward change. They are upbeat about new ideas and tend to focus on the critical benefits of change. Unlike innovators, progressives tend to be more stable in their business acumen and show a track record of consistent change over time versus dramatic change with ups and downs. They tend to be well respected among the congregation and exude a gift of faith. Gathering progressives to brainstorm and foster ideas of change is a very important part of creating an environment supportive of change. Even more important is to develop the influencers within this group. Progressives alone are not sufficient. You need to pick those who are leaders within this category and recruit them to serve on the leadership team for the change movement. By their very nature, progressives will respond positively, which is vital at the beginning of any new vision. They will tend to spread the vision, create an atmosphere of support and excitement, and okay the process with their peers in the early adoptor segment, something which the innovators cannot do. These are the Joshuas and Calebs, the future leaders of the new wineskin. Bank on this small group to catalyze the change. Love them. Befriend them. Disciple them. Invest a majority of your time and energy with this group and at the same time, communicate with and befriend leaders in the other groups who can allow the change to happen but will not promote it.

5. Cultivating The Climate For Change: Growing up on an Iowa farm showed me the importance of developing the soil before you plant. No farmer would plant valuable seed by merely broadcasting it on unprepared land. He takes the time to plow, disc, harrow, fertilize, and sometimes irrigate. Only then does he carefully sow, also giving it careful attention to soil type, timing and hybrid. Then if he's "lucky," he has a great harvest. Organic leadership takes into account the social climate surrounding the need for change. Some environments are more receptive than others to new dreams and ministry visions. A leader's job is to prepare the soil to receive and welcome the change. My friend, Gene Appel, who came to a very traditional congregation of 450, invested nearly eight years in changing the corporate culture before fully implementing changes. Central Christian Church is now a culturally relevant, outreach-oriented congregation averaging over 4000. At Scottsdale Family Church where I pastor, change is a common occurrence because this church is a new plant which was decidedly change-oriented in its inception. Because of its personality, people are suspicious if we do not change something every few months—if not weekly. Even then, leadership decisions must be based on the ability of our people to respond to changes. Most changes are rarely spontaneous, but must be intentionally strategized.

How does a leader prepare the church to accept change?

A. Preach and teach the basics which underlie the need for the changes. The beauty of church is our ability to educate people on the biblical grounds for evangelism, worship, and effective discipleship. By taking our basic beliefs and focusing on them, we can then illustrate how we are not accomplishing them with our current methods. Thus, we legitimize the new way if it accomplishes the ageless principles which are biblically supported and hard to reject.

For example, the need to reach the lost is an ageless truth, no one can deny. But is our church doing that? How many people have come to know Christ in the last six months; six years? Have they become fully functioning people within our church? If not, why not? Who is reaching these people today and what are they doing that we are not? By avoiding the focus on form and method, you start with the "hard-to-argue-against" importance of evangelism.

B. Educate leaders with books, tapes, and speakers who sow new thoughts. We grossly underestimate the ability of people to think for themselves. We sometimes rush the process when we speak the need for change without letting the influencers process the need themselves. By going through a cutting-edge book on contemporary ministry, various articles on the same, and audio and videotapes in leadership meetings, we repeatedly cast the vision for new thinking. A great approach is to bring in a consultant or expert who can often say the same thing you are saying with more power and effectiveness because he is an outsider with nothing to lose.

C. "Come and see for yourself." That was not only an apostle's recommendation to his brother, but is the single best way to catch a vision—witness one into existence. I've heard countless testimonials of lay leaders who attended a Willow Creek or Saddleback conference and walked away with an understanding of—no, a yearning for—what was happening. Visions are better caught than taught. Would you rather go to Hawaii or watch your neighbor's video of Maui? Besides the conferences, take in regular services of congregations accomplishing what you hope to pursue in your congregation. There is just something about sensing the energy in these bastions of hope. You may not buy into their methods or styles entirely, but you can seek to replicate it in your own way. Going as a team vs. sending individuals is pivotal. The after service/conference lunches and coffees offer key opportunities to root the vision and say, "Wouldn't it be neat if our church was able to accomplish something similar? We can. Let's try!"

6. Strategy Regarding the Change: Effective leaders intuitively know when to move ahead and when to pause. Managerial pastors nearly always pause too long and underestimate the possibilities in implementing change strategically. It is almost as if strategy becomes their main pursuit versus the change itself. Process is important, but it must not become the front burner issue. In other words, you start with the what and the why, not the how. The vision and need for change always determine the strategy.

With "cold turkey change," a pastor strives to bring about transformational change in a very short time. Conventional wisdom is that a new pastor should take plenty of time to understand the people and culture before suggesting anything different. Actually, this is often in opposition to change. A new pastor and staff can launch new visions because people are preparing themselves for something new, especially if it is exciting. Just as the body produces adrenaline to help it respond to stressful situations, organizations prepare themselves during times of transition and are often most open for change and new ideas with new leadership. Pastors who wait too long to implement new ideas sometimes lose windows of opportunity. The Columbo approach to leading has its wisdom. In this approach, a new pastor acts naive and tries things differently "because he doesn't know any better." Before you know it, the people like it enough to allow more change. Seize the momentum of a new congregation or transition in leadership. This is maximized when the new pastor is granted permission by the board and leadership during a thorough candidating process. Don't hold back. Don't hide your dreams and visions because you want the job.

If you suddenly seem to have hidden your agenda, the response will be to reduce support for your new ideas. Many people respond poorly to cold turkey change when they feel they have been betrayed during leader selection and when they have not been adequately prepared to understand and receive the change. Horror stories abound so that a congregation becomes guarded, even though the people have never witnessed a poorly executed vision themselves. I have seen congregants leave other churches where unpopular changes are being made and begin talking about their woes to those in the new congregation. Then when the new congregation begins discussing similar changes, it is almost immunized against the change. When cold turkey change fails, it is almost always a problem of process versus product (outcome sought). Ineffective leaders who do not have a good grasp on who the influencers are and where they stand, may as well shoot themselves in the foot. Autocratic and insensitive leaders mess it up for the rest of us who would bring about changes in our congregations. Nearly all horror stories are about ineffective leaders and leadership, not bad ideas or the need for change.

While cold turkey, out-of-the-chute change can be very effective if the leader is seasoned and strong, probably the most productive form of change is evolutionary versus creationistic. Evolutionary change is about gradual growth toward a specific style or paradigm. The big difference between leaders and managers is that the former are very intentional and clear on the intended outcome. The latter tend to perceive that managerial processing, such as changing computer software or implementing micromanagerial decisions is toward positive change. In general, the larger and slower the ship, the longer and harder it will be to turn. An object in motion will tend to remain in motion, unless acted upon by some other force. That other force is the leader, internal restlessness, attendance and financial statistics, external change, and . . . God. Every church is different and requires a unique response regarding speed and direction.

The most promising strategy for most churches is to adopt the menu ministry as described by Joe Seaborn in a previous chapter. When a congregation makes room for new ministries which focus on reaching new people, it is most apt to preserve the heritage of the past while making room for the future. Congregations which disallow room, budget and energy for new types of need-filling ministries quite often have attitude problems that need to be addressed prior to moving forward. The bottom line is that people with free will can deter a leader from implementing changes. Moses could not get the people into the Promised Land. They were not ready. Jesus could not convince Judas what He was really about. That's the power and challenge of leading. Some churches may be better off to sponsor an outreach ministry done in a user-friendly style so as to avoid the conflict of differing styles under one roof. Although unfortunate, this is better than nothing. At the same time, an off-campus worship service to reach the unchurched might be very wise, since newcomers might be turned off by socializing with more traditional churchgoers.

There is no right and wrong, because the proper response is a correlation between the leader's gifts and guts, as well as the congregation's readiness to adopt new change. Having seen the inside of some large, institutional type churches, I believe that there is much more support and readiness for change than most pastors perceive. The problem is that they are listening to the naysayers. The desire to be liked and accepted by everyone is a seductive temptation for the pastor who would be a change agent.

7. Affirming the Victories While Loving the Laggards: Just as a toddler needs affirmations for every new step, a congregation needs strong emotional support for small steps made in the right direction. The written and spoken word are powerful tools to reward risk takers, entrepreneurs, and change implementers. Foolish leaders tend to embrace those who align with the dreams and vision of the pastor, and alienate themselves from those who thwart the progress. Wise leaders understand that loving the footdraggers is just as important as encouraging the dreamers. When you alienate yourself from influencers who are early or late adopters or even laggards, you motivate them to deplete the energy behind the intended change.

Human motivation teaches us that the goal of persuasion is not to wholly convince a person to buy into a product or idea. The goal is to move the person at least a notch or two closer to the idea. A leader can often easily convince a progressive to accept the need to start a contemporary worship service to reach the unchurched. The pastor is silly to think he will ever get a traditional congregant to promote the idea. Rather, the real goal is to get the traditionalist to allow it to happen. By allowing it, there will not be the negative energy that is created when someone is against something. Go for the small victories. Be willing to sacrifice the things that don't matter for issues that do. I have a friend who said that he's going to get the pulpit off the platform if it's the last thing he does. It may be. There is a big difference between compromise and selling out. To compromise on something which is not that important is to make a concession, to show good will. To give up entirely on a ministry or program idea which will introduce the complacent congregation to a new way of ministry is selling out.

When small steps are made which introduce new ideas, fan the flames. Allow for an exhale, but don't stop. Pitch a tent; don't lay a foundation. Keep the momentum going. Just as the forces of inertia work against you when you are stopped, momentum is on your side once it begins. As the momentum increases, the organization becomes more and more resilient and less vulnerable to naysayers and laggards. Momentum to the organization is like adrenaline to the body. When a church gets going in the right direction, throw another log on the fire. Keep moving. As you reward the small victories and tell the tribal stories of parishioners who are responding well to change, people have a way of getting caught up in the new thing. In some ways, creating change in churches is difficult. In other ways, it is so simple that we overlook what it takes to change while searching for a more complex solution.

ENDNOTES

[1]Everett M. Rogers, *Diffusion of Innovations* (New York: Free Press, 1995).

Chapter 14

Church Plants

Effective Church Planting
by Robin Wood

Why Church Plants Fail
by Alan E. Nelson

*I*f we have any hopes of being strong in the 21st century, we must be about planting new churches, aggressively and effectively. Too many old wineskins exist to contain the new wine. If history tells us anything about organizations, it shows us that change comes hard. It is usually easier to give birth than it is to raise the dead. Religious organizations, like most others, tend to become ingrown, status quo, and accustomed to bucking change rather than welcoming it. If for no other reason than to stay alive, we must be about starting new churches.

By starting new churches, we significantly increase the chance of expanding God's Kingdom, not just rearranging it. Church planting is the best proven method for reaching the lost in North America. Before we help people discover second and subsequent works of grace, we had better relearn how to help them experience the first one. We've learned a lot about how not to start new churches. The horror stories of church plants that didn't make it are a dime a dozen. Nearly every district has at least a couple of worst case scenarios available in short-term memory.

The enemy then uses these to hinder future attempts at what should be more effective church starts.

As we learn from our mistakes, we must not waste our hard knocks. Starting churches in new fringes of growth where new churches are needed is strategic. Just as tactical, though more threatening, is to begin new churches of contemporary style in communities near sister churches which are not effectively reaching the unchurched among certain people groups (i.e. busters, Hispanics, blue bloods). If we do not position ourselves for more and better planting, we risk near logarithmic decline as aging congregations die for lack of change and relevance in a fast-changing society. This chapter includes ideas from two experienced church planters. Both have started new churches from scratch and have studied the field of church planting for years.

Robin Wood is the founding and senior pastor of Mountain Park Community Church in Chandler, Arizona (Church of God Anderson). Robin is pure energy. One peer laughed when I brought up Robin's name. "You know him? Why even Ritalin doesn't quiet him down." Quiet or not, Robin has led an impressive church, growing it from zero to an average of 1000 in Sunday morning worship over 10 years. Seventy percent of these worshippers were unchurched. At the time of this writing, Mountain Park has just moved into the initial phase of its first permanent church facility, having worshiped in a high school the first decade. Most of Mt. Park's growth has been evangelistic, reaching the unchurched through contemporary music, drama, and life-relevant messages from the Bible.

Effective Church Planting

The question is often asked, why start new churches? Whether we are casting vision to plant churches from a local church, a state or district ministry, or from a national church initiative, we must answer the question. Why plant when we have so many churches presently that are not viable? Shouldn't we come alongside a struggling or plateaued church and strengthen what already exists, instead of starting new churches? Statistics show that new churches have an unusual capacity to reach the unchurched person who doesn't know Jesus Christ. New church plants have an extremely large percentage of conversion growth.

That reason alone is sufficient for us to boldly cast the vision for assertive church planting.

The answer to the question of why I personally should be a part of a church plant came to me from God's Word. Every pastor that plants a church must have a direct vision and mandate from God. Planting a new church is not just a nice idea. Phrases such as this don't cut it: "It seems like the thing to do." "I'd like to give it a try." "Sounds like fun." "I'm frustrated in my existing church, so maybe I should go start a new church." "Every denomination is doing it." "Church growth experts say it is the best way to reach the lost." Ten years after birthing Mountain Park Community Church, I find myself telling other church planters, "If you can avoid the call, do so at all costs." Why? Because if you do it well, starting a new church will take every ounce of emotional, physical, and spiritual strength you possess. In fact, it will take more than you've got.

The motivation to plant a church must be a vision from God and his Word. You cannot adopt a vision from another planter or great leader. You cannot cast another's vision, no matter how powerful the vision. You must own the vision. The vision must grip you more than life itself. Then you must be able to cast the vision time and time again until a remnant of God's people own it with you.

God's Vision for Me

In May of 1987, God gave me the vision for planting a new church in the Mountain Park Ranch/Foothills area of Phoenix, Arizona. Late one night in my Casper, Wyoming home, I couldn't sleep as the dream of starting a new church gripped my thoughts. In less than two months, we would be moving to Phoenix. My passion for helping people find Jesus Christ had been at the forefront of my ministry as an associate pastor. Through music, youth, and evangelism, I had watched many come to Christ in established churches. I began asking God to give me a vision through his Word.

I never dreamed I would find my personal vision in the book of Revelation. These messages were for the Early Church. I had read them many times, but when I came to the message to the church in Philadelphia, time stood still. The words leaped off the page. They were no longer words given to the church nearly 2000 years ago. They were words given to me for the new church in Phoenix.

"To the angel (pastor) of the church in Philadelphia (Phoenix) write, These are the words of him who is holy and true, who holds the key of David. What he opens, no one can shut, and what he shuts, no one can open. I know your deeds. See, I have placed before you an open door

179

that no one can shut" (Revelation 3:7-9).

My heart warmed. I began to cry. The phrase "open door policy" popped into my mind. It was God's promise to me for Phoenix. "Robin, I place before you an open door that no one can shut." The open door was a promise to me that many would come to know Jesus Christ as their personal Savior. For the next several weeks, I began to search the Scriptures to discover what this open door policy meant to the early church. This was a promise to open a door to ministry. The Apostle Paul would often refer to a door being opened for him time and again as he planted churches and took the gospel to the lost. Paul talked about this in Troas, Ephesus, Philippi, Corinth and other places. In Athens, the door was not open and few responded to the gospel. The Book of Acts describes what happens when this Open Door Policy is in effect.

Acts 19 provides a foundation for the Open Door Policy. What happened in Ephesus is a picture of what can happen in a church plant. Paul was put out of the synagogue, the established church of his day. So Paul had an idea which I call "The Church Planting Idea." Paul took the disciples and rented the public hall of Tyrannus for the next two years. He began holding discussions about Jesus. Historical study reveals that Paul rented his public hall during the normal siesta time. Word spread concerning these discussions. Paul argued persuasively, reasoned from the scriptures, and proved to the listeners that Jesus was the Messiah. The Open Door Policy and Church Planting Idea provided the fundamental principles for our new church in Phoenix.

Jesus said, "I have placed before you an open door that no one can shut." The Holy Spirit is drawing people to God's salvation. The fields are ripe unto harvest. But the workers are few (Luke 10:2). Our responsibility is to strategically reach these people as Paul did in Ephesus.

Starting Mountain Park

We decided that one of the best ways to get the news out about this new church would be via the telephone. In five weeks, we were able to make 23,000 calls. We first asked, "Are you already actively involved in a local church? If they answered yes, we thanked them and asked them to pray for our new church. If they answered no, we asked a second question. "Would you allow us to send you mailers describing our new church and announcing our first worship service?" If the answer was yes, we simply verified their name and address.

From this first step, we developed a mailing list of over 2300 households. After four mailings and follow-up phone calls, we held our first public service on October 18, 1987, with 305 attending and twelve making first-time decisions for Christ. During the first year, over 100 made decisions for Christ and we averaged 179 in morning worship.

The only motivation that would cause me to ask people to make 23,000 calls and send out mailers was The Open Door Policy. We cast this vision to every phone caller. Every time we picked up the phone, we were praying we would come into contact with someone God's Spirit was already touching. We believed the promise. The strategy resulted from the vision.

Knowing that many people are ready to discuss and meet Christ in a neutral, nonthreatening context, we thought of places conducive to beginning a church. Public places where seekers could hear discussions on Christ are schools, hotels, libraries and similar sites. We began in a high school auditorium.

Because the vision has never changed at MPCC, we continue to find ways to penetrate our community with an invitation and a safe place to come and discuss eternal things. Presently, over 900 gather on any given Sunday. Over 2500 refer to Mountain Park as their home church. Since MPCC is a safe place to discuss and seek, the church continues to grow. We use personal invitations, mass mailers, door-to-door questionnaires, and special Friend Days. We have been willing to start two new worship services. One is called Hot Church and the other is The Gathering. Hot Church is a worship service for students, grades 6-12. We put a contemporary service together with our young people. Our youth pastor speaks to their needs each week. The students are involved in presenting the dramas, singing on the worship team, and playing in the Hot Church band. Five years after starting Hot Church, Sunday attendance of students went from 25 to over 200. The Gathering is a midweek service with a Bible study format, ending with a question and answer time for informal discussion.

What Does It Take to Plant a Church?

Who can plant a church? Should I start a new congregation? These are questions I am commonly asked. In the first year of starting MPCC, I thought that everyone should plant a church. Ten years after Mountain Park's birth, I am much more sober in my encouragement. I have often wanted to write a Top Ten List of what it takes to plant a new church. There are a number of excellent publications and church planting toolkits available. Yet, these materials are also often complex. After years of planting and assisting other church planters, let me cut through the complexities and give you the bottom lines necessary for a church planter.

If you want to be a church planter you must be able to . . .

1. Cast vision with passion and zeal for the lost.
2. Raise money.
3. Communicate with excellence in your preaching and teaching.
4. Raise money.
5. Recruit leaders.
6. Raise money.
7. Train leaders.
8. Raise money.
9. Build a quality pastoral staff.
10. Raise money.

I have attended many seminars on church planting and have read most of what there is to read about the subject. What are the two most important gifts needed to plant a church? My answer is always short and to the point. First, the spiritual gift of leadership is imperative. Second, the church planter must be an exceptional communicator. If a person has been gifted by God in these two areas, the chances of success soar.

There is a basic gift/talent mix needed to plant a new church. It is imperative that you have the spiritual gift of leadership. Leaders develop followers. Since most new churches start from scratch like Mountain Park, you have to be able to draw followers from day one. You must lead in a way to gather a core group and then gather others. The spiritual gift of leadership is needed in every realm of starting a new church. To recruit and train leaders takes the gift of leadership. To build a strong pastoral staff takes the gift of leadership. There isn't a part of your role that doesn't require this gift. Raising money takes the gift of leadership. Planting a church without the gift of leadership is a mistake.

Casting the vision well and helping pre-Christians understand the Bible requires communication gifts. A planter is asked to gather a core group of people to believe in the vision of a new church. With no physical building, this new church has to develop a spiritual presence using rented facilities. In our case, after 23,000 calls, four mailers, a final phone call and an invitation to the first public worship, 305 people responded. A majority of these people had not been to church for 10-15 years. The church planter gets up to speak. If you ring the bell spiritually, people will come back. If you don't, you won't have another chance. In new churches, the pastor is the primary draw. We can spiritualize it. We can say the results are up to God. But the bottom line is that God uses people. The church planter must be exceptional and passionate at communicating the good news of Jesus. Hopefully, most of your attenders will be those seeking at a new church. Without passion and communication gifts, the church will not be able to hold those who come.

I have been involved in over 15 church plants, either directly or as a consultant. I have trained church planters. Without exception, the ones who succeed have only a few things in common. I have watched a number of church planters carry out all the right strategy, yet when the people came, they were unable to deliver the message with excellence. In every case, the church would not survive. I was involved in one church plant that had an opening day crowd of over 200 and yet today they run under 40. Why? This particular church planter did not have the spiritual gifts needed for leading and communicating.

The church planters who have succeeded have been able to cast vision. They are pure leaders and exceptional communicators. Beyond these foundational gifts and talents, the rest is up for grabs. You can be a poor administrator and still succeed. You don't have to be able to carry a tune in a bucket, but you have to express passion in your leadership and speaking.

Related to leading is the ability to raise money. It is not so much about money as it is trust. Do enough people believe in you to invest in you? Can you communicate a vision which motivates people to invest their money in the dream of a future church? If not, church planting is probably not the place for you. Without money, basics such as program staff, office expenses, advertising and all that goes on with funds will not happen. We don't lack for money; we lack for vision, because a big vision articulated well will attract the needed resources, if God is in it.

Why Church Plants Fail

A growing number of men like Robin Wood understand what it takes to begin a church from scratch and develop it into a self-supporting, vibrant, full-service congregation. Having begun two new paradigm congregations myself, both from scratch, I would concur with Robin's observations. While he listed the abilities church planters need to possess, I'd like to address ten of the most common reasons why plants fail. Over the years, I've gained firsthand accounts of numerous new congregations which have started in our greater community. In addition, dozens of other stories filter through the grapevine. While we hear about the supernova starts and learn about their successes in magazines, tapes, and even self-hosted seminars, you often fail to hear about the high toll paid by those who do not experience stellar effectiveness. We can learn most from our failures, if we humbly analyze them.

Many infant congregations toddle along, living off menial support systems, straining just to survive. Others pull in the shingle and close up shop, never to be heard of again. To see a potentially viable church fail is sad. You wonder whether it was God's will. Where was God in supplying the vision, the resources, and the people necessary to make a go of it? Why does He seem to bless some while others die in their shadows? The human side of watching congregations struggle and die at times means being tempted to quietly celebrate, because those who fail prove what you felt all along, that starting a new church is tough and risky. After you get beyond the self-centered feeling that you are somehow better, smarter, or more talented than the rest, it is helpful to consider just why it is so many new congregations never take off. Here are ten primary factors which emerge from most failed church starts, generally in descending order of impact.

1. Lack of a visionary leader. You need a clear, concentrated passion to start a church. The pastor must be a leader, one who is able to cast a preferred future, gather people and align them with tasks. Just being a pastor is not enough. Just being a pastor-leader may not be enough either. When a church starts from scratch, you need a pastor who has entrepreneurial gifts. The movie *Tucker* is a good example of a man with a dream to build a new car and who takes the idea from conception to finish. That same can-do attitude is a rare commodity among leaders in general. Entrepreneurs are high energy, self-motivated, innovative, and focused. These strengths can also be weaknesses if the pastor gets bored easily, fails to find managers with whom to partner, and comes on too strong for some followers. Nurturers rarely make good church planters. Teachers alone do not fare well. The traditional pastoral personality lacks the tenacity and visionary drive needed to begin a church from scratch. If you start a church with a good-sized core of people, it is not as crucial to have a strong entrepreneurial gift—but leading is just as vital.

Not only must the pastor have leader gifts, but he needs to have a spouse who has the vision as well. Ministerial life is demanding on a household, but planting is very difficult when the spouse does not have a complementary call. The sacrifices, risks, and lack of stability strain family life. If the home front is not united, starting a church will be an even tougher challenge.

2. Money. I had to laugh as I read Robin Wood's emphasis on money. Since we pastor in the same metro area, I happen to know he wrote the chapter while in the middle of their first big building campaign. But buildings or not, now more than ever, economics play an important part in determining the viability of a new church. In the past, starting a congregation with little to nothing was not an impossible situation. People were less consumeristic, more understanding, and at times more willing to give once they began attending the new church. In most communities across America, there is a sense that quality and service must be a part of any organization from the start. More than ever, a church plant needs the financial ability to hire both a pastor and a worship director, plus provide adequate publicity, signage, portable furnishings, and quality audiovisual equipment. All of this costs money. When you begin a church in a high rent area, the prices rise even more. Salaries must allow staff to live in the area of ministry, and publicity and equipment must allow for a level of excellence which those in the surrounding area will appreciate. The number one reason new businesses go bad is that they are undercapitalized. Why do we think the church is different? An adequate financial seed is needed to purchase the essentials which can attract participants who, in turn, will begin giving toward the church costs.

So many churches are still in the dark ages regarding business acumen. We would do better to put more money in fewer church starts and increase their odds of starting well. We should also have a cut-off point to avoid throwing funds at a work that never got off the ground. If a plant can't be on its own in 2-3 years, it probably is not going to be self-sufficient after 5 or 10. Some denominations do not allow budget credit for churches that help other indigenous churches get started. They are old paradigm in thinking. Beginning a new church designed to reach the unchurched is nothing more than a domestic mission. I do not think of myself as a pastor, which may be why I don't fit in a lot of the boxes, let alone the attire of my traditional pastoral peers. I think of myself as an urban missionary. Reaching the unchurched professionals of north Scottsdale requires a different way of thinking and acting than a traditional pastor. Why then don't we see new churches as urban missions and grant them the same status as any other missionary? The district which invested in the congregation I planted did it right. The problem in church planting is often not spirituality, leadership, or strategy, but merely economics.

3. Mismatch with Community. A pastor must mesh with his/her community. Socio-economics, education, and cultural preference are all keys to understanding a people group. Midwesterners often do poorly on the West Coast. Urban pastors are not apt to do as well in rural settings. Blue collar and less professional pastors should not take on a plant in an upper middle class suburb. Mother churches and denominational supervisors need to make sure there is a good match before providing a blessing and money. Too often we hope for the best and let good-hearted people fail because they just do not fit the culture they are trying to reach. Not only must the pastor match the community, but the church mission must target a group large enough to establish a congregation. If you are in a buster community, don't put together a church designed to reach boomers. If you are in an unchurched area, don't create worship services for established Christians. If people in your community listen to jazz and soft rock music during the week, don't feed them country western or classic hymns on Sundays. Matching the community has to do with a missionary mind-set. We cannot assume that all churches in America are the same. They require specific strategies and appropriate pastors. The church we planted in southern California has struggled since we left. I did not know how difficult it was for that district to find someone in their ranks who matched the culture of that church and community. Matching well is crucial.

4. Lack of Cohesive Core. Planting a church is a bit like building a snowman. You need the right kind of snow (ripe environment), but you must also begin with a tightly packed snowball before you begin rolling. Making the snowball is equivalent to developing a core group. Coming to town, putting up your shingle, and expecting people to show up on Sunday is ridiculous. You must first get a core of people who will carry the vision, bring their friends, serve in ministry roles, and hopefully give financially. If you are beginning with an existing Bible study or spin-off group from a mother church, spend plenty of time with them to see if they are compatible with each other and the dream. A Baptist church near us just failed in a church plant, partly because their core group consisted of very sweet, traditional, older people. They were beginning in a school located in a brand new community with many young families who were not traditional.

If people are not on the same page and/or if they do not get along well among themselves, starting will be tough. If the snowball is not packed well, it will crack when you try to roll it. Our second church plant started so much easier and faster, in part because the core we were able to gather seemed more cohesive, similar to each other, and was larger. The best way to start a church is with a healthy group of 150-200 from a mother church. If you start from scratch, make sure you have 30-50 committed people minimum, before you go public with an outreach service and advertising.

5. Mediocrity. The temptation for planters is to promise more than can be provided. I have seen several congregations mail very attractive, four-color brochures, promising a contemporary, excellent program for all ages, even from the start. Unfortunately, most of them do not deliver. Once you attend the service, you find a nursery which is poorly staffed and inadequately equipped, greeters who are not overly friendly, and a service which may be good, but lacks the dynamics implied in the publicity piece. In most subcultures in the United States, mediocrity is unacceptable, whether it is inadequate sound, sloppy music or transitions, bad drama, or an uninspiring message. You only have one chance to make a good first impression. Many churches fail to communicate excellence in what they do and turn people off to further involvement. It is best to communicate a vision, a classy presentation of an attitude and mind-set, but not promise more than you can provide.

Better to have less and well done, than too much poorly done. Do not start a new ministry until it can be staffed and presented professionally. Figure it will be a five-year process of building the infrastructure so as to help people understand the long-term direction. Most people have never helped plant a church and they are tempted to think of their former congregation which had established programs in place for years. Provide a few classy touches, like publicity, audiovisual equipment, apparel, and a professional exhibit, to drop hints that you are quality and know it when you see it. This will give consumers confidence that, although you are just starting, they can count on future improvement as resources increase. You don't have to have it all together from the start, but unless there are viable hints that you are headed that way, people are not apt to wait around until you get your act together. Professional signs, informative displays, trained greeters, teachers, and worship leaders in addition to drama and messages, all communicate excellence which attracts people. Best of all, it keeps people who, in turn, invite their friends—the best way to grow. The greatest compliment people can pay you is to tell their friends and neighbors about their new church.

6.   Poor Start. Sprinters tell us that the race is won or lost in the starting blocks. This is often true of church plants. Getting the team on board and the foundation laid are crucial. Since you only have one chance to make a good first impression, you'd better do it right the first time. Planters who want to move into a neighborhood and start a service right off the bat are almost always doomed to fail. Get a lay of the land. Know the area, the people. Find adequate meeting space. Network, advertise, and develop a core group. Don't underestimate the importance of the "getting going" phase. The getting going phase precedes the core group development phase, which has more to do with networking people and casting the vision, all the while you're raising funds to start with a bang. These first two phases may take 6 to 12 months. The first public service needs to be big, exciting, and pretty smooth. Have your core people meet beforehand a few weeks to practice together and get used to each other and the new facility. You might try preview services, once per month, to allow people to sample your style and talk it up among friends.

Poor starts are also created by waiting too long to launch. I received good advice in my first plant from a seasoned pastor. He said, "If you want to plant a small group, start with small groups. If you want to plant a church, start a public worship service." Building community among the core is crucial prior to going public, but if you wait too long, you're apt to blow your inertia as well. Many people will not join a small group because they are more threatening. They want a larger gathering to test drive a new church. Your Sunday morning service is your flagship, around which the other ministries will form.

Churches which do not begin with a bang and gain momentum quickly are not likely to survive in today's world of heavy economics and change. The grapevine will spread the word if you are an "up and coming" church to be considered or a "wanna be" congregation not likely to make it. Often, if a church has not established itself well within the first 2-3 years, it is best to pull the plug and start over with a new name, new leadership, and maybe even a new core group. Like a rocket taking off, the initial lift-off takes a lot of thrust. Social gravity is working against you.

7. Target Too Obscure. Who are you trying to reach? Just as no radio station plays a little country, a little classical, a little hard rock, and a little jazz, no church can reach all people. You'll go out of business. God calls every congregation to fill a niche. That is why a lot of our territorialistic ideas on not wanting sister churches too close to us is ridiculous. We could park next to nearly any Nazarene or holiness church in our state and not compete, because we're after a different market than they are. Our specific goal is to reach unchurched, boomer men in north Scottsdale. We figure that if we can crack those tough nuts, we'll be able to get their families and other fringe people on board as well. That also means that when well-meaning Christians come to our church and want us to become a clone of their previous parish, we lovingly suggest they find another congregation.

If we truly strive to be all things to all people, we become nothing to nobody. A Willow Creek model is not the only successful way to reach people. If you want to attract older Christians or those raised in a conservative church, model after most holiness churches. If you want to reach younger, unchurched people, be different. The key is knowing specifically who it is you want to reach and then you won't be bothered by losing those you're not aiming for. When those you are trying to target come and go, then you have to ask yourself some tough questions. It is ridiculous for us to say we want to win everyone in the northeast valley for Christ. That is not our calling, nor is it anyone's specific calling, but it is the cumulative call of all the churches in the northeast Phoenix metro area. Define your target. It will set the tone for everything you do. Fail to define your target and you'll wonder why you don't hit anything.

A focused target also means you will define your niche within the larger faith community. God is not redundant. He places different churches in the same community to reach a variety of people. Although we do not like to admit it, there is a degree of competition among churches. When you are the new kid on the block and your ministry is bold and reflects quality, your chance of taking off increases significantly. For years we ministered in the shadow of Saddleback Valley Community Church. My office was less than two blocks from Rick Warren, whom I consider a friend. Rick says that churches do not compete with each other, but with the world. I agree with the theme of this statement, but then, Rick never tried starting a church in the jet stream of Saddleback. We were unique from Saddleback, but close enough in style to feel the presence of a larger, more established seeker church in the community. In Scottsdale, we have families attending our church from other church plants that are not fairing as well. The big church locally is Scottsdale Bible Church, but their gift is teaching while ours is evangelism, so we complement but don't compete with them. *Doctrinal differences should not be the primary rationale for planting.* Few people today attend a church due to its theological distinctions. They are interested in leadership, philosophy of ministry, and style. When seeking a community in need of a new church, we need to look at what we can uniquely offer.

8. Too Traditional. Unless you are developing a church in a retirement community, why would you begin a traditional church? There are dozens of them already existing in most communities. The best way to reach the unchurched is to develop a seeker-oriented service and complementary ministries which will attract and hold pre-Christians. Willow Creek is known as the seeker-model, but like we said, it is not the only model for reaching the unchurched. Paul said he became all things to all people in order to win a few. Too many pastors from traditional backgrounds develop new churches from their comfort zones, instead of thinking in terms of reaching the unchurched. We must think like a missionary. The largest single percentage of people making up new churches are those with Catholic and mainline backgrounds who gave up on church as adults. They are willing to return to a church which is culturally relevant, practical, and user-friendly. If you provide a service that resonates with life in the 1950s-70s (as most of our churches do), you will not attract or keep those who have given up on traditional, organized religion. Our goal is to expand the Kingdom of God, not just rearrange it. When we draw people from other churches, we are not necessarily evangelizing. Less than 1% of churches are growing primarily from evangelistic endeavors, that is, reaching the lost. Traditional ways worked in previous decades, but rarely work today.

9. Lack of creativity. Telemarketing works for some. It failed for us. People in our community despise phone solicitation. They want to pursue their own shopping patterns. We've tried Friend Days, brought in celebrities, offered Mrs. Field's cookies, joined the Chamber of Commerce, rented a bunny suit and offered a live Easter bunny visit to parishioners who host Easter egg events in their neighborhoods, did shopping mall concerts, contacted media for multiple news items, created a promo video to send to 10,000 families in our area and for attendees to give to their neighbors, hosted marriage and parenting seminars and yo-yo contests for kids, brought in snow at Christmas (in Scottsdale, Arizona), sponsored pool parties, youth rallies, concerts, picnics, and on and on.

Innovation and creativity are key elements in getting a new church up and running. When you beat the same drum so long, you'll run out of momentum. When something works, use it, then try something else. When something fails, try something else. There are thousands of methods we can employ to communicate the one vital message—God loves you and has a plan for your life. At Scottsdale Family Church, attending is fun and engaging. At least that's what we like it to be, so we keep trying new things. Most unchurched people consider "fun church" an oxymoron. We strive to give them what they need, but in a way they like. When a church keeps God in a small box and does the same thing over and over, you will rarely be able to generate the enthusiasm and excitement necessary to grow a new church. The initial energy to get a church going is tremendous, and requires doing all you can to create enthusiasm, sustain interest, and raise momentum.

10. Lack of Tenacity: Ministry is challenging, period. Church planting may be the most challenging ministry in some ways: you're working with people who are new to Christ, who do not think in terms of Christian priorities, and who will let you down. Finances are almost always tough. If you're like most new churches, you're working in temporary facilities and the wear and tear of set-up and tear-down seems endless. Add to this the fickleness of new believers, the sense of being all alone in ministry, and the spiritual warfare of engaging the enemy on the frontline, and you sometimes want to give up. Nearly all new ventures are exciting at the start, but soon comes the reality phase—where you face the challenges with not much of a track record and certainly no guarantees for success. If perseverance is not a character trait of yours, you will probably not make a good planter. Too many people call it quits too early in the planting field. They give it a good shot, but not their all.

We must be planting more and better churches, whether it be district ventures, mother church births, or partnering. The key is finding entrepreneurial leaders who, with mentoring and resourcing, can quickly start healthy congregations. We must intentionally increase the numbers of plants in new and growing areas if we are to reach the lost in America, let alone finance the reaching of the lost abroad in the future.

Chapter 15

Church Daughtering

by Wayne Schmidt

*T*he first work of grace must become our first priority. Church planting is the best known way to help people find Christ. We have to plant more and better churches if we are going to stem the tide of those closing after the turn of the century. New communities require new churches, and new churches are the best way to reach the unchurched. We have yet to come up with a perfect model for doing this. Much of our approach has been hit-and-miss. This may be the only way to create new faith communities . . . any way you can. Sometime ago I was talking with the leader of the Vineyard movement a few days after its founder, John Wimber, died. Over 500 Vineyard Fellowships popped up in the last two or three decades, but their goal is to start 1500 more. When I asked about their attrition rate, he responded that "only 1 or 2 out of 5 don't make it." Considering that other movements lose 3-4 out of 5 starts, that number is pretty low. He said, "You need to know that planting new churches is a part of our DNA; it's a large part of who we are."

If we are to improve the rate of new churches becoming viable, fruitful faith communities, we must develop a womb from which these new churches will be born. District and general church planting is a bit like test tube pregnancies. You can still birth new bodies, but it is not the *natural, nurturing method. The best way to begin new churches is via mother churches. In daughtering a new church, an existing church takes a risk, but the benefits can be outstanding. There are other ways of daughtering a church than investing people and money. Recruiting, training, mentoring, and other support measures can help church planters become successful. It would seem that most churches are more into self-preservation and Kingdom building than they are giving others life and Kingdom building. Granted, a large percentage of a congregation's resources go back to itself up to the size of 300, which includes most of our congregations. This leaves it up to our larger churches to model church planting, or to encourage syndicates/alliances of smaller churches to work together in this effort. The goal of Scottsdale Family Church is to help start 25 churches in our first 25 years. These new babies will not just happen; they will be intentional offspring, reflecting who we are as a church. An optimum future strategy would be to inject general, district, and private monies into mother churches designed to reproduce themselves.*

We need more leaders such as Wayne Schmidt, senior pastor of Kentwood Community Church (Wesleyan) in Michigan. Since its start in 1979, the church has grown to over 2400 in weekend worship services. Kentwood has daughtered three congregations and plans for more. One of the churches Kentwood helped found is represented in one of the chapters of this book, Daybreak Community Church (Wes Dupin). Wayne is married to Jan and is father to Chris, Jordan and Elise. He is author of **Soul Management,** *co-author of* **Accountability,** *and holds a D.Min. from Trinity Evangelical Divinity School.*

I remember the nervous feeling. Were we really ready to be parents? Had we made the decision too hastily? How would our future be different because of the commitment we made to give birth to new life? No, those weren't the thoughts running through my mind as Jan and I anticipated the birth of our children. They were the thoughts running through my mind as our church participated in giving birth to new churches.

I believe in the impact of new churches. New churches reach new people. New churches try new things. I also believe that the most effective way to give birth to new churches is a healthy local church becoming a parent. A local church knows the unique characteristics of its community and can lend credibility to a fledgling new church. Our church has played a part in the birth of three churches. Two have blossomed and are reaching their communities for Christ. One never survived infancy. We've known the joys of success and the heartache of failure. If you're looking for a risk-free way to extend the kingdom of God, don't get involved in church planting. But if you believe new churches are worth the risk, then choose to become a parent!

Preparing the Parent Church

The health of the mother during pregnancy can directly affect the health of the child. She should practice the positive behaviors—healthy diet, proper rest and exercise. These factors make a difference during the pregnancy, influence how emotionally prepared the mother is to relate to her child, and how quickly she will recover from pregnancy. The same is true for a mother church. Good preparation of the parent church contributes to a healthy daughter church. The better the mother church is prepared, the more emotionally and spiritually ready it will be to relate to the daughter church in a positive manner. A well-prepared mother church will more quickly recover from the temporary loss financially and numerically that accompanies the birth of a daughter congregation. Your church may never feel completely prepared for the adventure of becoming a parent—but take heart, most parents don't!

Creating the Vision

Only fervent prayer with hearts that break for lost people will develop a burden for church planting. If the vision is a result of the latest ministry fad or passing impulse, it will evaporate when the necessary sacrifices become apparent. New churches result from the direction and conviction of the Holy Spirit created in prayer. This vision is most often hatched in the heart of the senior pastor. It begins with a paradigm shift—when a pastor not only senses a calling to serve a congregation, but also to reach a whole community for Christ. I am grateful to serve Kentwood Community Church as its pastor. But I am committed to building a great church to reach our city for Christ, not to reach our city in order to build a great church. That distinction is crucial! For the pastor who feels called to build one congregation, giving away people to begin a new church is seen as a step backward. The pastor who is called to reach a city will see it as a step forward. To permeate a city of any substantial size will require multiple congregations and locations.

To reach greater Grand Rapids will require a strategic vision that captures two dimensions. The first is that our local church will grow as large as God intends in order to make a regional impact. Large churches are not better than small churches, but they are different. They provide opportunities in worship and programming that can effectively reach unchurched people. Second, reaching our metropolitan area for Christ requires the establishment of new congregations. We will not reach the half a million residents in our county from one large church. Factors such as driving distance, sociological boundaries and preference for the strengths a smaller church offers make new congregations a necessity.

The way to reach a large community is not *either* a large church *or* planting new churches. Reaching our community involves *both* a large church *and* new churches. Therefore our vision is to plant a new church every two years, encourage one hundred people in the congregation and through their contacts, to form the core of the new church. Our church has grown each time we have been in the process of birthing a church. In addition to planting a church in our community every two years, our goal is to participate in alternate years in planting a church somewhere in our nation or world. Planting churches in our community will primarily involve the contribution of people and credibility; planting new churches elsewhere will primarily involve the contribution of financial resources.

Cultivating the Climate

Creating a vision statement is one thing—preparing the congregation to receive it is another! Announcing the decision to plant a church in the weekly newsletter or from the pulpit is an unlikely way to generate support. The key word is *ownership*. People must sense the burden for church planting in their hearts and not just as something on the pastor's heart. The process for ownership is different for every congregation, but the following ingredients help create the climate:

- The senior pastor must share a sincere and heartfelt burden for church planting. He should encourage the congregation to pray for the possibilities of church planting.
- Develop one-to-one meetings with key, influential leaders in the congregation, seeking their input and ownership.
- Create a task force to develop the strategy and necessary steps for new church development.
- Involve, involve and involve the members of the parent church. This includes a challenge to be part of the core group, making referrals of people who live in the geographic area of the new church, praying for the specific needs of the project with each strategic step, and giving money or other resources needed by the new church.

- A thoughtful process of congregational awareness, including the following questions:
  - ▲ Who should know about the project first, then second and so on, so that the right "ripple effect" of vision is created?
  - ▲ What communication vehicles should be used? Possibilities include the newsletter, special brochures, platform prayers and announcements, small group discussions, and video presentations to name a few. When should these approaches be utilized?
  - ▲ How will the congregation be initially informed and updated regularly?

Ultimately, the Holy Spirit creates the climate conducive to church planting. Just as the vision is the result of prayer, the climate is the result of prayer and planning. The Holy Spirit moves our attempts in creating climate from superficial manipulation to supernatural motivation.

Developing a Strategy and Timeline

What begins with vision and continues with creating the proper climate must ultimately translate into specific timelines and activities. These vary greatly, depending upon the congregation. Each pastor or task force must match timelines and activities to the customs and structure of the mother church. Flexibility must be maintained with careful planning becoming the basis of changes, not the guardian of preconceived ideas. The greater the planning, the greater the opportunity for well-conceived responsiveness and spontaneity. The strategy and timeline should include:

- Decisions to be made and when
- Necessary communication with the congregation
- Items to be done in conjunction with the denomination or overseeing body

Once these are mapped, they should be reviewed and updated as the process unfolds.

Denominational Relationship

If the project is in partnership with the denomination or overseeing entity, certain issues should be discussed and resolved prior to the public phase of the church planting project. Two of our church planting endeavors have been in conjunction with the West Michigan District of The Wesleyan Church. Like any partnership, certain items must be clearly specified.

First and foremost was the selection of the church planting pastor. The pastoral leader of the new work is the most critical dimension of new church survival and success. In our case, our local church has been responsible for the selection and screening of candidates. We then present our choice to the district leadership for final interviews and approval.

Second, where does the authority for supervision of the new church rest? It is important that the church planting pastor have one supervisor—either the sponsoring church pastor or the denominational official. In our projects, the District Superintendent was selected as the supervisor. As pastor of the sponsoring church, I served as advisor, cheerleader, and prayer partner—but not supervisor. This arrangement worked well in the church that succeeded, started by a pastor who required little in terms of supervision. It was *tested*. In our church planting effort that failed, some of the core group that came from our church viewed my lack of intervention as a lack of interest, because they did not understand my role. By the time they understood they were to look to the district superintendent for help, it was too late.

Third, the financial arrangements were clearly specified. The denomination provided funds directly for up-front expenses, but by the end of the third year, their subsidy ended. Our local church provided people who were encouraged to tithe to their new church family from the start. The district leadership established the pastor's salary and the pastor of the new church worked with the district in developing the church budget. Again, I played an advisory role.

Fourth, a name for the new church needed to be selected. The final choice of the name belongs to the church planting pastor and people. In our case, the denomination only stipulated that the word "Wesleyan" be in the title. The rest was up to the church planter.

A fifth issue was the church's relationship with other Wesleyan churches in the area. Unfortunately, many local churches can be very territorial, assuming they have franchise rights to a geographical area even if they are not effectively influencing their surrounding community for Christ. While some sensitivity to other existing churches must be exercised, people must be reached. If one local church is not making an impact, another may need to be placed within a few miles of it. This can actually encourage growth in the existing church.

Agreements in these and other areas must be very clear. Fuzziness can lead to misunderstanding and disharmony at very critical stages of new church development. This tension will have a chilling effect on the current church planting effort, as well as potentially jeopardize future cooperative efforts.

Church planting is not only a courageous undertaking for a sponsoring church, but for a denomination. They must be willing to face failure. We have experienced success in two of our three church planting efforts. I view that to be a pretty good batting average, but people who need to succeed every time would be disheartened by the one that failed. Church planting is *risky* for everyone involved—the church planter, the core group, the mother church and the denomination. Those who are adverse to risk had best find a safer way to extend the Kingdom. I believe there is a relationship between risk and reward—between faith and fruit.

A denomination must also struggle with the reality that new churches rarely play by all the rules. By nature, most church planters are pioneers. They love uncharted territory. New churches do not have years of history at church camps and denominational gatherings. Their loyalty must be won. If a district has forty churches and five of these are fairly new, it is a very different organization than a district with forty older, established churches. Church planting not only grows a district, it changes it. Change and risk are not for the timid.

Planting the Church

Most of this chapter relates to the mother church. Every church should ask two questions. Are we located in a sizable city (50,000+ or having bedroom communities more than 20 minutes from our church)? Has God blessed us numerically, so that we've grown beyond the 200 plateau? If the answer to these questions is yes, you should prayerfully pursue parenting a church. For too long, the primary strategy has been targeting communities where holiness churches don't presently exist. Proximity to one or more healthy holiness churches can provide credibility for the new church and a source of fellowship and support for the church planting pastor and people.

Beyond a healthy birth mom, the planted church must have the right leader, surrounded by a core group that shares the leader's vision, and matched to the right target area.

Selecting the Target Area

Within a sizable city, there are several distinct areas that can be targeted by a new church planting effort. These communities may be distinguished by geographical area, ethnic identity, cultural characteristics, economic levels and lifestyles. The mother church must see the metropolitan area through an understanding provided by a history of its development, demographic data, transitions it is experiencing or projections for future growth.

For a first church planting project, choose a target area that is similar to the community in which the mother church is located, but separated by some driving distance. Planting a church in a similar area is more likely to succeed and initial success can be important to openness for future endeavors. Learning basic principles through experience in planting a church in a similar setting will prepare a mother church for the unique challenges of church planting in a cross-cultural setting.

Recruiting the Core Group

"Caring enough to send the very best" is an appropriate guideline for a mother church as it prepares to give away a core group. This does not mean necessarily uprooting people who are presently fully developed in their gifts and abilities, but certainly people who can potentially develop into leaders of a new congregation. This is not the time for the mother church to unload its disgruntled or dysfunctional people by encouraging them to join the new church. The mother church should exercise discernment in who it encourages to be part of the core group. Much of the eventual growth of the new church is related to the quality and cohesiveness of the initial core group. Issues to be explored include:

- What motivates these people to be part of the new church?
- Do they sense a call to reach the target area for Christ—particularly its unchurched people?
- What is their track record? Are they servants or power-hungry; flexible or inflexible?
- Are they in agreement with the new church's philosophy and strategy?
- Will they participate financially (where your treasure is, there will your heart be also) and by serving in ministry in the new church?

It might be helpful to develop a "ten most wanted list" of characteristics of core group members and use this in helping to screen people. In our church structure, we can neither send people nor prevent them from going, but we can encourage or discourage people to be part of the new work.

Besides a quality issue, there is a quantity issue. Our goal as a mother church is to establish new churches that can grow to several hundred people. Critical to that growth potential is how long it takes for a church to break through the 200 barrier. If a church can break this within a few years of its beginning, its ministry and fellowship structures tend to reflect those of a larger church. Our desire is to get them halfway there right from the start, to provide a core group of 100 people, which in our case is less than 5% of our congregation. We ask those in the core group to make a two-year commitment. At the end of two years, if they feel led to return to our church, they will be warmly welcomed and their involvement will be celebrated. They are welcome to continue their involvement in their new church home.

Selecting the Church Planter

Since a new church has no identity, no history, no building and limited resources, the leadership of the church planting pastor is crucial. Strong, effective leading is crucial. Our church began in 1979, when little information existed about how to select a church planter. (Some might say this is obvious since they chose me!) In recent years, many organizations have improved our understanding of the makeup of an effective church planter. Since there are many excellent resources available, let me briefly summarize what we look for in a church planter.

An effective planter has a holy heart, passionate for a vital relationship with God. Integrity and humility flow from the core character of a person who has been cleansed and then called by the Holy Spirit. A church planter is better off to have a personality higher in dominance and extroversion. These characteristics are more naturally conducive to making the decisions and building the relationships critical in a new church launch. Among the planter's spiritual gifts should be leadership, faith, and teaching or prophesying. These gifts will enable the development of both the organizational and communication dynamics to cause the new church to grow.

Experience and educational background must also be weighed. The best indicator of future performance is past performance. The desire to lead a growing church is one thing, and it is quite another to have actually led one. If a person's past ministry has not stimulated growth, it is less likely that his future ministry will. What has been his vision in the past and how did he communicate it? Did he rally a team around that vision? Did he solve the problems and make the changes that come with growing ministries? Were people won to Christ and discipled in the faith?

In the unique arrangement of the mother-daughter relationship, it is also necessary to have a level of trust and compatibility between the church planter and mother church pastor. Keeping this relationship free of jealousy and infused with mutual appreciation will help it withstand the inevitable probing that will come as people "test" their opinions of each other.

The Sacrifice Is Momentary; The Satisfaction Lasting

Our involvement in church planting has enriched our church. It has prevented us from concluding that the great work God wants to do can be contained in our local church. It has purified our vision for evangelism by leading us to spread the gospel in ways that may never show up in our local church statistics or budget. Even when one of our daughter churches failed to thrive, we learned that it is dependence upon God, not our strategic plans, that brings success. It's not our power or resources, but God's Spirit that breathes life into a new work (Zechariah 4:6).

Recently, one of our daughter churches celebrated its eighth anniversary. They invited me to speak and share in the joy of what God had accomplished through them. I was overwhelmed with emotion to think that a small sacrifice years ago (sending less than 100 people) resulted in an ongoing ministry with an attendance of nearly 1000 that is seeing over 100 people coming to Christ each year. What a return on our investment! And not only do we have the joy of being a parent church. When our daughter churches fulfill their vision of planting a church, we'll get to be a grandparent!

Chapter 16

The Role of the DS/Bishop in the 21st Century Church

by Keith Wright

*S*ome would believe that we are now in a post-denominational era, where the general and regional structures are obsolete and unnecessary. Although we are convinced that the nature of the regional and general church structures must significantly retool along with the local church, it is too bold to say they will cease to exist. Organizational nature, whether mosaic or contemporary, instructs us about the need for coordinating supervision when you have a certain number of bodies involved. In sales there will be district/regional managers. In corporations there will be middle and overseeing managers. It only makes sense that such a position will continue to be a part of organizational church life.

While some of us in the trenches are familiar with the jokes about wanting and not wanting to be a district superintendent/bishop, we need to take a look at the emerging role of the 21st-century apostle. Too often we have assumed that just because a person is effective in a local church, he should be elevated to a managerial role. Unfortunately, we have lost some of our best practitioners to non-frontline ministry and hamstrung the district office with someone having different gifts than those needed for the job. Sometimes the person who gets elected is a person who is politically correct, a non-boat rocker, and although amiable, is not likely to set the district on fire. I overheard one businessman remark during an election, that he wished for a campaign speech from the candidates to hear their visions for the organization. Why do we elect a person whom we have not heard in terms of district or general church vision and passion? These and similar questions may daunt our traditions in the future. Where are the women superintendents, bishops? Why not elect a proficient lay person to oversee the region? What can we do to raise the benchmark for district supervision and leadership vs. management?

The old paradigm leaves the role as predominately managerial, filling holes, putting out fires, and administrating district budgets. The new paradigm requires the district leader to be just that, a leader of leaders; equipping, training, motivating, casting vision, and teaming up with church pastors and lay leaders to maximize their potential. One example of this new paradigm leader is Keith Wright. Keith has been the superintendent of the Kansas City District Church of the Nazarene since 1990, coming from the senior pastor role of Kansas City First Church. Fifteen new churches have been planted in the district under his leadership, and three more will be planted by the time this book is published. Keith has worked hard to get himself out of a traditional managerial role and into one of leading leaders. The district office is more of a resource center than administrative hub. In addition to serving on numerous boards, he is husband to Liz, father to Lori and Stacey, and grandfather to Cori Elizabeth and Kelly Nicole.

The Role of the New District Superintendent is to provide transformational leadership that will recognize, promote, and inspire the fulfillment of the great commandment and great commission with excellence through healthy churches.

Living in the Supernatural. The new leader of the 21st century will live on the cutting-edge spiritually. The spiritual experiences of the past will serve only as markers for the future. The day-to-day ministry of leadership will be fresh and up-to-date because of a daily encounter with Almighty God. Prayer and fasting will be the normal way of life in order to lead with authenticity.

Phone calls and personal conversations with pastors and laypeople will often end with a time of prayer. All that is done will find its root in a dynamic walk with God. The normal way of life for the district leader will be to believe that solutions will be found, dreams will come true, and miracles will take place. The district leader will truly be a "prisoner of hope" and will constantly communicate what is more important in the church than budgets, buildings, numbers, or programs. Top priority is experiencing the supernatural presence of God. Bill Bright, founder and president of Campus Crusade for Christ, suggests at least six things to cultivate the supernatural presence of God: (a) think supernaturally; (b) plan supernaturally; (c) pray supernaturally, (d) love supernaturally, (e) seek and use the supernatural enablement of the Holy Spirit and (f) believe God for supernatural results.

When the supernatural presence of God is being experienced, numbers, programs, and money become very exciting. God is close and situations that seemed impossible become possible. People begin to believe in a miracle that comes from the hand of God. Energy and life are always pumped into a church when the supernatural crowds its way into every activity. The encouraging leader must fan this flame of expectancy, moving to where God is at work.

A recent 24-hour district pastors' prayer retreat brought the following response:

- Renewed sense of God's presence.
- Effective cleansing of debilitating sin, error, faults, etc. through confession.
- Strengthening of inter-pastoral bonds through honesty and transparency.
- Renewed sense of dependence on God.
- Deeper awareness of the Holy Spirit's activity and power among us.
- Empowering for more effective rather than merely efficient ministry.
- Inner healing in pastors' hearts and lives.

- Modeling of first-nudge obedience to the Spirit's leadership during the retreat.

One pastor remarked: "My prayer life has been revitalized and so have I." When we operate out of a renewed passion for God, we are able to see, feel, and respond positively to the ordinary events of life, where God is able to perform His supernatural miracles. Neil Wiseman wrote, "The contemporary church already holds what it needs in its hand . . . ecclesiastical power, gifted personnel, competent leadership, impressive facilities, prestige, respectability, money, and organization. But it needs one more thing . . . a supernatural empowerment of all its personnel at every level and I mean every level."[1] Could it be that the apathy in our churches today is simply a result of refusing to make "the main thing the main thing"? "As never before, the contemporary church needs the renewed, invincible fire of God at her spiritual center, to make her a redemptive instrument for converting the world to faith in Jesus Christ."[2] As district leaders, we must fan the flame of genuine righteousness. It cannot be administrative business as usual. Could it be that Almighty God is standing on tiptoes in Heaven, looking for leaders who will courageously lead pastors and laypeople into the supernatural realm of ministry? Two thousand years ago, a group of ragtag nobodies believed in Jesus Christ and miracles began to take place in and through them. The Holy Spirit energized and thrust them into their world. Lives dramatically transformed and changed.

The prayer of Henri Nouwen should be that of every district leader:

> "Lord, let your Spirit give me power
> to overcome all hesitation,
> to take away all fear,
> and to remove all shyness.
> May your Spirit help me
> respond gratefully to you,
> speak freely about you to everyone I meet,
> and act courageously to let your Kingdom
> come."[3]

Shifting from position power to people power. Writing rules and policies as a denomination grows is easy. In order to be **more efficient**, we need organization, but this is also what causes us to be **ineffective**. We can be driven by the policy rather than the vision to win and disciple people in Christ. Control can easily become more important than permission to get on with ministry. Jesus and His disciples did not get along well with the established religious people of their day, and no doubt they would not make it with some of us. We have often heard the following comments by those more interested in control than a transformational ministry:

"We have never done it that way before."
"We tried that before, but it didn't work."
"No one does that in this church."
"We don't do things that way."
"It's too radical a change for us."
"If only it were that easy."
"When you have been around longer, you will understand why it can't be done."
"How dare you criticize what we are doing."
"We have been running this church long before you were born."
"Who gave you permission to change that?"
"What you are suggesting is against our policies."
"Won't that open us up to liability?"

The climate must allow "yes" to be said more than "no." A new paradigm is emerging for the 21st century. Leaders who are leading pastor-leaders will seek ways to encourage, resource, equip, guide, and release these pastor-leaders to move into ministries that have the potential of being more effective. This means giving permission to fail. We learn from our mistakes and our failures. It is the responsibility of the district leader to encourage the development of a "new thing," even if mistakes are made along the way. This is where trust comes, believing in people beyond what they see in themselves. The responsibility of the new district leader is to provide a climate where the highest potential of every pastor can be developed, giving him or her freedom to test and experiment without reprimand. There will be encouragement to dream huge dreams, even if it has not been done before.

At the very heart of the permission-giving relationship is trust and love. Love lets go and allows people to stretch and develop at their own pace. When district leadership has a high level of respect, trust is the result. Out of trust and love, grace abounds, and God can work in powerful ways. The new 21st century district leader will lead from relationships that flow out of trust and love, not from position.

Leadership that is proactive rather than reactive. Denominational leaders of today often find themselves in a reactive mode. We will have crises that must be dealt with, but is it too easy to blame others? We can blame the seminary for not training pastors to be true leaders. We can look at the denominational system and find fault with it. Of course, we can look at our culture and say that the reason we are in trouble is because of it. Pastors and lay leaders blame the fact that people are not committed as they used to be. Money is a big issue and it is convenient to point out that we just don't have enough or that the denomination is asking for too much from our budget. If all else fails, we can blame the church down the street that has a more charismatic pastor and is growing.

We can always find something to react to, but maybe it's time for denominational leaders to begin moving in a proactive direction. Move out of the heavy administration and begin to be a consultant for the local church. This means spending time in evaluation with the people in the church, as well as training and equipping them for future ministry. Most laypeople want the best for themselves and for their church. They want to make a difference. The problem seems to be that they do not know how to make that difference and allow themselves to rest solely on the paradigms of the past. A new district leader will begin by helping them change their old paradigm to a new ministry paradigm. Part of our problem is that our training has been predominantly with pastors and not with laypeople. As the district leader and a team of district personnel work with a local church, including laypeople and pastoral staff, reinventing the local church to be a dynamic force for God is then possible. This means helping laypeople take off their blinders and begin looking at their people differently, as well as how they "do church."

One of the responsibilities of the new district leader is to create a climate of optimism by which laypeople and pastors can move toward solutions. This will not happen by making pronouncements of the future in denominational gatherings like General Assembly or District Assembly. It will be most effective as a district leader is involved in one local church after another, via training, equipping, guiding and directing. The district leader will serve as a consultant in local churches and also put together a team of consultants who will work with him.

The primary ministry for the district leader of the future will be to bring resources and needs together—whether that is locating the right pastor for a local church, finding people to put a new roof on a little church, or training and equipping people for ministry in the 21st century. The district leader must have the courage to step up to the plate and declare to the local church, "Hey folks, that path won't take you where you want to go. I want to help you find the road you need to travel that will benefit you and the Kingdom of God." When we move into a proactive role as a consultant in a local church, the trust increases and the entire district and denomination is perceived as valid in the mind and the hearts of laypeople in the local church.

The second area for being a proactive leader is to actively promote the starting of brand-new churches. This means constantly casting vision to pastors and laypeople about the value of starting new churches. There is nothing more exciting than giving birth to a brand-new, baby church. The responsibility of the district leader is to assess and train potential church planters and work with an existing local church to determine the community in which this new church should start. If starting new churches takes place in America, it will be as a result of local churches dreaming the dream and then marching forward to plant them. The district superintendent will want to help them be successful, such as having monthly meetings to equip and train church planters and resource them for effectiveness.

Another area of vital importance for the district leader is selecting strong pastoral leadership. Psalms 78:72 says, "And David shepherded them with integrity of heart; with skillful hands he led them!" Every church and community is unique. There was a day when most of the churches were about the same. They sang the same songs, gave the announcements at about the same time, and organized their churches in about the same way. The schedule of services was about the same in every church. This is no longer true. The district leader must work with the church board to discover the uniqueness of that church and its needs. The next assignment is to research and find the potential pastor that will match the needs and uniqueness of the church. This is where the ball game is won or lost in district ministry. The new district leader of the 21st century will not be afraid to work with the entrepreneur. He will stay close with encouragement, but will release the creative leader to do the work of ministry and build the church God has in mind. Sometimes pastors are labeled as being rebels, when in fact they are truly gifted by God to be an entrepreneurial kind of person who breaks new ground and moves into new paradigms. We need to look for a "loyal rebel." When we have fear of working with this kind of a person, we reduce our organization to mediocrity.

How do we finance the operation? Districts in the future will employ people who are charged with the responsibility of raising money and starting non-profit businesses that will create a stream of income for ministry. The normal budget system will probably not be strong enough to support an aggressive church planting and revitalization program in the district. Money follows mission. This means that the district leader must be skilled in casting the vision so that they want to be a part of it. The question is, how do we get the job done? Often we think in terms of having enough money to hire personnel to do all that needs to be done. As we move into the 21st century, we will discover more and more retired people, skilled and trained by businesses, who are looking for another place to make their lives count. We will begin seeing more and more people who have been active in Sunday school and lay ministry move into the pastoral role as laypeople. There will be hundreds and thousands of retired persons who would be willing to give themselves to ministry, either as part-time or full-time lay ministers on a church staff. This is a new resource that we must tap.

As I look to the future, I am very optimistic. We need to resist the temptation to add to the structure and restructure our denomination. We need to continue to push the ministry to the grassroots where people live and work. The ministry is in the local church. There is no church except the local church. The only reason for the district and the denominational headquarters is to serve the local church so it might be effective locally as well as globally.

The John Wesley model for leadership is the order of the day. For thirty-three years, Wesley went to the fields to do his preaching. The reason was because the people would not come to the church building. He is quoted as saying, "If you don't like field preaching, learn to like it!" After John Wesley's many years of open-air preaching, he confessed: "To this day, field preaching is a cross to me. But I know my commission and see no other way of preaching the gospel to every creature."[4]

George Hunter III says, "Both of the Wesleys were pragmatists and would do whatever it took to reach people for Jesus Christ. Charles was a cultured poet and musician with high church aesthetic taste, but he shelved his preferences, condescending to write hymns to the tunes of low-browed drinking songs being sung in England's public houses!"[5]

Wesley was in the people business and not the church politics business. Hunter says, "Wesley believed that all church policies and structures should be judged by whether they facilitate or frustrate 'the work of God' and the 'spread of the true religion.'" He saw the parish system as frustrating the Great Commission and therefore, declared that, as one called into apostolic ministry, 'I look upon all the world as my parish."[6]

This great 18th-century spiritual leader was driven by the Great Commission and taught his growing army of lay preachers as follows:

> "You have nothing to do but to save souls. Therefore, spend and be spent in this work. And go always, not only to those that want you, but to those that want you most.
>
> Observe: it is not your business to preach so many times, and to take care of this or that society; but to save as many souls as you can; to bring as many sinners as you possibly can to repentance and with all your power to build them up in that holiness without which they cannot see the Lord."[7]

John Wesley believed in the principle of multiplying units in order to reach people and to disciple them. He said: "Preach in as many places as you can. Start as many classes as you can. Do not preach without starting new classes." He developed strong lay leaders by giving them the responsibility to be class leaders.

In reading the life of Wesley, it appears that he was a church growth specialist and believed in church health. For example,

- He developed a strategy for outreach and discipleship.
- He was constantly observing classes, societies, towns, hecklers and detractors, leaders, parish churches, persons, and crowds.
- He insisted that the ministry be practical and meet the needs of the people.
- He moved toward receptive people although he preached to all people.
- He encouraged indigenous ministries in the multiplication of units.
- He believed in seed planting by sharing the Good News and letting people think about it before they were challenged to accept Christ.
- He reached across social networks to people.

Our Wesleyan-Holiness heritage has given us an excellent theology and spirit by which to minister. It is time for us to rediscover the passion of our founding fathers and to "exegete" the culture God has given us. This is what our founding fathers did. They also gave the message of holiness in the language, the music, and the culture of the people they were attempting to reach.

This can be the greatest day for us if we will once again become a spiritual movement! Our theology is exactly right. What our people need to hear is that God can transform lives and fill them with His holy love. Churches, old and new, can come alive if we dare to follow the John Wesley Model.

George Hunter III said, "We do not honor our founders by blindly perpetuating in a changing world what they once did, nor by hijacking their tradition and imposing something culturally alien; we honor them by doing for *our time and culture what they did for theirs.*"[8]

ENDNOTES

[1]Neil Wiseman, *The Untamed God,* (Kansas City: Beacon Hill Press, 1997), p. 124.
[2]Ibid., p. 124.
[3]Henri Nouwen as quoted in *The Untamed God,* p. 125.
[4]John Wesley, *Journal*, Sept. 6, 1772.
[5]George Hunter III, "Reaching Unchurched People," Nazarene Theological Seminary Seminar, Jan. 1993.
[6]Wesley, *Journal*, June 11, 1739.
[7]Wesley, *Works*, Vol. 8, p. 310.
[8]Hunter, "Reaching Unchurched People."

Chapter 17

The Role of the General Church in the 21st Century

by Keith Drury

*M*ost of us have opinions when it comes to our general church structures. As effective organizations grow and expand, the tendency is to create structure and management to stabilize and perpetuate the new growth. Unfortunately, most organizations invest more and more of their resources into the perpetuation of themselves vs. the things that help create them. The process is called institutionalism. The Wesleyan heritage movement has seen significant growth in its early years. The holiness movement specifically is one of the few American-founded religious movements. But time is catching up to our success. We are now seeing the results of institutionalism, where we will either die or make significant changes that *will allow for transformation. Many books dealing with organizational ad hoc-racy, reinventing the corporation, and re-engineering, address the prevailing climate in our denominational centers.*

If we are to survive, let alone thrive, in the 21st century, we will have to transform our general church structures. Doing business as usual will not cut it for long. Incremental evolution will be like arranging deck chairs on the Titanic. Whether the change is economically, spiritually or culturally driven, we cannot stay as we are. What worked in the past will not work today or tomorrow. Beating yesterday's drums a little louder is not enough to exorcise the demon of impotence and the ineffectiveness of our structures. While many propose we are living in a post-denominational age, the idea of providing kinship, accountability, and familial networking still seems appropriate.

Therefore, instead of suggesting we put to death our central church structure, we believe there is a place in the 21st century for a new and different denominational presence which will do what the local church cannot.

Keith Drury has looked at the general church structure from inside and out. Keith is currently a religion professor at Indiana Wesleyan University. He has invested a good amount of his life within general church positions and has remained prophetic in style. He is a graduate of Princeton Theological Seminary and has received two honorary doctorates. His writings are included in more than sixty books, manuals and booklets on ministry and Christian education, and he has published over 300 articles. His popular "Tuesday Column" can be found on the internet. Prophets are not always liked and can be blamed for diagnosing problems which others prefer to deny, but there will always be a place for such people in God's Kingdom. Keith enjoys being a husband to Sharon and hiking around the United States.

About 20 years ago it was popular to talk about the "demise of denominations." One well-known author even published a book announcing their death. Of course, he was right to a degree. And like an aging, old woman gathering plastic bags for her "final exit," some denominational leaders started downsizing toward death, enabling a self-fulfilling prophecy. On the other hand, denominations, including the holiness denominations, are still around after 20 years have passed, though they have far less punch than they once had. Perhaps they have a different punch today. What has happened to denominations in the last two decades or so and how has that affected the role of the general church in the holiness movement? What factors in the local church affect the general church?

I.   The Influencing Factors

One cannot examine the role of holiness denominations in the 21st century until we know where we are and from where we've come. Those who ignore the past and present cannot predict the future. Where have we come these last 20 years? What are the realities of holiness denominationalism? How has the landscape already changed and with what factors do we contend? Why is it that many holiness church members do not show the same loyalty we took for granted in the past? Here are nine factors:

1.   New Generations

The research keeps showing that Baby Boomers and Busters/Xers have far less "brand loyalty" to denominations. At first this alarmed denominational loyalists. It encouraged local churches which reaped a harvest of quite a few Lutherans, Reformed, Methodists, and charismatics who were willing to give up their former brand and join holiness churches. It has a greater effect on the denomination than the local church. The casualness of these Boomers, who are now on the board and into leadership, is affecting the general level of the church.

2.   Transfer Growth

Holiness churches still see people saved, but the proportion of conversion growth to transfer growth has changed. An increasing number of our members are transfers and have not been saved "out of the raw." They came to us after attending another denomination. Many of the transfer members did not get saved at all, but oozed in with a testimony about present faith, and not a specific, datable conversion. First-generation converts saved off the street tend to be more loyal to their denomination than transfer members. Transfers may salute the denominational flag, but don't sing the Star Spangled Banner robustly. They split their loyalties among several denominations, their present and former ones.

Transfer members often retain some loyalty (and doctrines too) from their former denomination. Today, people choose a church on style and atmosphere, not doctrine. They usually look for a church "like the church where we lived before." By this they usually mean the "feel" or worship style of their favored former church. They wind up in a Nazarene or Free Methodist church which "feels just like First Lutheran, where we came from." They like the services, but they keep their "first wife" in their heart still. They are loyal, but loyal to two denominational spouses.

3. Diversity

A Big Mac is a Big Mac pretty well anywhere in the country and around the world. But a Nazarene is not a Nazarene anywhere you go. Neither is a Free Methodist or a Wesleyan. People discover this when they move to a new town. Perhaps they attended the local Free Methodist church in New York and loved the services. They move to Pennsylvania and look up the local Free Methodist church, expecting to find a similar church. Are they ever surprised! When they write to their former pastor, they say, "We found a church exactly like your church—it is a Baptist church." They are right—except in doctrine (and one cannot say that for sure). They are likely to find greater similarities between their former Free Methodist church and their present Baptist church than they did between the two churches with the same brand names.

We have always had diversity, but it is broader today. As people see this diversity, their desire to support the common cause declines. They are willing to be loyal to the Wesleyan church, but they are not sure what a Wesleyan is. Members like this (and sometimes pastors too) will sometimes admit they have a greater common cause with certain churches from other denominations than with their own. This is especially glaring among the super churches, where there seems to be greater common ground and shared mission with other super churches outside their own denomination than with the smaller churches within their own denominations.

4. Second-Generation Christians

The children of denominational loyalists have their own loyalty, but usually at a less intense level than their parents. As holiness churches have raised up new generations of Nazarenes, Wesleyans, Church of God Anderson, and Free Methodists, they are loyal to the denomination, but not with the loyalty of their parents, especially if their parents were saved off the streets.

5. Political Distrust

The dominant American political value-shift of the last quarter century is a distrust of central authority. Even today's Democrats sound more conservative and small-government-oriented than yesterday's Republicans. Big government is bad and decentralized state's rights are good, period. In the last twenty years, the conservative, anti-big government mood has prevailed among holiness churches. In many Sunday school classes, small government decentralization is as sacredly held as holiness (and perhaps a more common topic of conversations). Holiness people, along with most other Evangelicals, have come to believe that national headquarters are wasteful bureaucratic centers, the work of which should be done nearer to grass roots. They assume even more waste from international centers (i.e. United Nations). It is a difficult day to be in the denominational headquarters, when leaders get painted with the same brush as Congress and the White House.

6. Tax Cut Fever

Though the desire to cut taxes is an extension of the political mood, it deserves its own listing. Americans believe that central government spends too much money, requiring local folk to pay too much in taxes. Both Republicans and Democrats have sounded the call to cut taxes and give relief to the frontline taxpayer. Most holiness church people think it is a good thing to lower the obligations to national entities and invest the money at the grass roots, where it will be spent most efficiently and for the best things. Can they divorce their assumptions about political government from church government? Many church leaders hoped this value would be confined to politics. Their hopes were not realized. Most local church members take a similar view on denominational obligations as they do on taxes. "We should pay less so we can do the real ministry of the local church at the grass roots." They refer to their denominational obligations as taxes when speaking to each other.

7. The Rise of the Super Church

In the last 20 years the number of holiness churches over 1000 has increased. For example, in The Wesleyan Church for the first time churches have appeared which owe in excess of $100,000 for district/conference and general obligations. While 15% of less is less, and 15% of more is more, it is shocking when translated into dollars. When the church's obligation reaches a full-time salary of a staff member, most laity begin asking questions about this obligation. Some super churches wonder if they need a district or headquarters. Many take a do-it-yourself approach toward the things a denomination used to provide. They no longer limit their pastoral search to their own denomination's schools or even churches. Senior pastors say they get little help filling staff positions from the denomination and they sometimes feel that their own printed materials are superior.

The super churches have changed the picture forever. Some holiness denominations have considered or passed adaptations of "maximum taxes" on a church. When the church's obligations reach a certain point, they quit paying budget on the rest of their income. In some cases, the super churches have become publishers and programmers, providing to smaller churches the resources and training traditionally supplied by denominations.

8. Parachurch Influence

Parachurch organizations have existed as long as the holiness denominations, but their power has never been so mighty. The church growth movement swept through the holiness churches in the 1970s and 1980s with such might that parachurches began to influence local churches more than their own headquarters. Denominational leaders were often playing catch up. They once had an almost exclusive franchise in leading their people. There were camp meetings, training events, denominational programs, celebrations and denominational distinctives which people dutifully accepted. People didn't need to go to Promise Keepers; they had General Conference. As much as 90% of the influence on local members came from their own denomination. Denominations controlled much of what their people heard, read, which speakers they hired, programs they sponsored and doctrine they believed.

This day has passed. Individual members today have better access to all kinds of influences beyond their own denomination. While a loyal denominational member of the past might pick up some books at an independent camp meeting, or may have subscribed to an independent magazine, most of the influence on this member in the 1950s was from his denomination and local church.

The average member has access through TV and radio to Robert Schuller, Charles Stanley, Chuck Swindoll, Pat Robertson, Jan and Paul Crouch, or Jim Dobson every single day. That doesn't even count the influence of the internet, where a growing number of non-holiness organizations like *www.bible.org* give away resources and curriculum to holiness churches which teach from them, oblivious to doctrinal differences.

Most of the parachurch leaders have written books which have become the staples of many churches' Sunday school classes, once dominated by denominational curriculum. Denominational leaders have tried to head off the use of nondenominational curriculum, but eventually softened their warnings by marketing the same authors they formerly warned against, sold through their own publishing houses. Holiness people now excerpt these non-holiness writers for chapters in our own topical studies. We figured that if the grass roots want to study such writers, we might as well be the one selling it to them. The result is selecting the bland and doctrinally non-offensive writings.

You can't blame them. The extraordinary growth of the local Christian bookstore and direct marketing has given the individual Christian access to a virtual plethora of books and music influencing how he or she thinks. Denominational materials now have to compete with all kinds of materials nearer to home. The internet has arrived with broad access to a world full of (often free) materials. Denominational (and independent) publishers are now sent scrambling again. There are more nondenominational influences on today's holiness churches than ever. This affects loyalty to the general church level.

We have YFC, Campus Crusade, Navigators, InterVarsity, Day of Discovery, Bill Gothard, Bible Study Fellowship, InJoy, SonLife Ministries and dozens of others. What about Promise Keepers? This exploding parachurch organization may have accomplished in a few years what denominational officials could not do in a century with men. New organizations are birthed daily. Among the ministerial students I teach, more than half declare their eventual intention to start some sort of parachurch organization and do itinerant speaking, singing, or consulting work. Where did they get this? It is no wonder they come to college with such a dream. In the last twenty years, that seems to be where the action is. There are thousands of holiness men more loyal and dedicated to Promise Keepers than they are to their own denomination. All of these organizations now provide conventions, programming, materials, and more importantly, leadership training, which denominations once supplied.

9. Generic Soup

The distinctions between denominations is not as sharp as it once was. Calvinists have moved a bit toward us and we have moved to meet them, near the middle. Same for Catholics. Holiness people no longer believe all Catholics go to hell or that Lutherans all need saving. We've eased up on our distinctives, trading for a sense of unity with the larger evangelical and perhaps, mainline churches. The flavor of our soup doesn't taste much different than the others. Local members don't see that much difference anymore. Why should they be more loyal to their own denomination than any other? "Aren't we are all saying the same thing?" they ask.

II. The Coming Changes

What will be the role of the general church among the holiness denominations in the future? Can it survive? How will it function differently than in the past? Is there any role for the general church in the future if these trends continue? There are at least six critical roles for the general church:

1. Discipline

Sometimes pastors go bad. They cheat on their spouses or swipe money from their churches. Who will step in? Dobson? Though not a romantic assignment, intervention and accountability are necessary. The denomination which fails to discipline its pastors' sins will eventually collapse and probably should.

Discipline is especially critical with the advent of the super church. There are some situations where a super church is so large, and contributes so much money to the district, that removing the pastor threatens stability. If such a pastor commits adultery, the temptation to leaders is to ignore it or cover it up. The temptation is to figure out a way to provide a quiet and temporary low-grade discipline which leaves the pastor in his position. This way he will keep the people tithing and the denomination from having to pick up the huge debt his leaving would cause. Denominational leaders deserve our prayers and support in these situations.

While such discipline is largely the function of a district in the holiness denominations, we all know who sets the standard, limits, and advises the superintendents, and who carries through on the disciplinary policy: the General Superintendents. We hope for spiritual and moral revival in the 21st century. If it does not come and things go the way they have been going, such discipline may be one of the primary roles of the denomination in the 21st century. It will take guts. The denomination which cannot maintain a moral ministry deserves to disappear.

2. Prophetic Scolding

Who will step in when the church is headed the wrong way? Paul Crouch? Any ministry directly dependent on donations will be careful to avoid unpopular positions with its supporters. Here is where the "tax" system pays off. Denominations must generally please their members or they too will lose support, but it is not so immediate and dramatic as in parachurch organizations. (One insider reports that when their TV ministry took the prophetic trek their income took a 40% nose dive in one month).

Who will stand and say embarrassing truths about the Church of God Anderson, Wesleyans, Free Methodists or the Nazarenes? Who will scold us for our materialism? For our lusting after the gods of success? For our tendency to lie about numbers on our reports or build our own ministerial careers? Who will call attention to our self-satisfied churches who care little for the lost and have arranged the entire church budget to provide comfort for themselves? Who will say the hard things a church needs to hear? Who will give the correction? Who will provide the rebukes we need from time to time? Don't expect to hear them from TV. If we hear these words at all in the 21st century, my hunch is it will have to come from bold denominational officials who care little about vote tallies, income or popularity, but who are willing to scold their churches when they need to hear the truth. This is a definite role for denominational leaders in the 21st century. It won't be about "packets and programs," but about this kind of leadership.

3. Education

Though denominational Bible colleges, colleges and universities no longer have an exclusive hold on training lay people and ministers in their denominations, the denominational educational industry is so large, so powerful, and has so many votes in conferences, it will likely continue to be one of the major ministries of 21st century holiness denominations. The Free Methodists have a low-cost plan of support, but some argue that education is the number one priority of Nazarenes and Wesleyans. Training ministers has always been one of the last things a denomination gives up. Most of the attempts by super churches to supplant this work have fizzled. A denomination that cannot train its own ministers usually ceases to be a denomination or is only pretending to be one.

4. Pensions and Loans

If the so-called Xer generation has its way, a denomination's primary role will be with pastors, not the laity. Nowhere does this become more critical than in the maintenance of a sound and funded pension program under the stewardship of leaders in which pastors have total trust. The financial scene has changed. Individual responsibility has emerged in the last decade and the assumptions that a denomination should not care for its ministers is dying. The rising assumption is that a denomination should help ministers use part of their income to provide for themselves. As we approach the 21st century, an increasing number of denominations will opt for IRA type options where ministers feel some control of their own retirement funds. Denominational pension plans are giant funds and the Boomers who have amassed hefty amounts in these denominational funds will retire in the second decade of the 21st century. If the fund is a good one, they will convince upcoming generations to come of its value. This is certainly a role of the general church. A fund may arise which joins several holiness denominations together.

There are also loan funds. One of the success stories of denominations has been these revolving loans. Though they are sometimes criticized for rates as high as banks, or for refusing loans to shaky churches, generally they have been a sound success for denominations and will probably play a major role in the 21st century. What many church officials could not do in new churches through advice and promotions, they now can do through loans. The big finance role of the general church will not diminish, but will grow in the 21st century.

5. Speciality Publishing

The power of evangelical denominational publishing houses has been sliding for decades. The independents have cornered some of the market. The diminishing loyalty factor hurt denominational cash cows like curriculum sales. When the Church of God Anderson publishing venture collapsed, other holiness bodies were alarmed. Free Methodists had already quit printing, but have kept up publishing. (Even the Southern Baptists, America's largest denomination, does not print). Wesleyans made an alliance with David C. Cook to sell Cook curriculum, adapted a bit toward the Wesleyan position. Nazarenes launched heavy efforts to retain local church loyalty and reach out to market to non-Nazarene churches. The last decade has been one of turmoil for holiness publishers.

Any denominational publisher who made a profit (among non-profit organizations called "revenue in excess of expenses") in the last ten years should be affirmed and rewarded handsomely. Witness the internet with free and minor fee resources, where the local church becomes the printer of materials produced and posted on the internet, often with little or no doctrinal examination at all. General publishers face rocky waters in the 21st century.

Who will publish specialty resources? Will Gospel Light make good membership materials for Nazarenes? Will David C. Cook produce solid books on holiness for Wesleyans? Will Zondervan help Free Methodists teach their views on communion or women in ministry? Not likely. In the 21st century, we may see general church publishers reverse their trend of going generic to sell to a broader base and, instead, get more specific. Like cable TV, they may narrow cast their products to a denominational niche, instead of trying to sell a watered-down product to Baptists. Whatever they do, it will be a big challenge. Publishing specialty resources remains a vital role in the denominational church.

6. Leadership

There is still a role for denomination leadership in the 21st century. It will be shared with Promise Keepers and other media individuals, but it will still be there. Leadership will have to be earned, not entitled. Wisdom and boldness will increasingly be the characteristics we want from our general leaders. Being a general leader in the 21st century will take guts— for the work will at times be messy. It is no job for preachers who want prestige, power, or high pay. It will require boldness to tell the church what it doesn't want to hear, with the broken heart of a weeping prophet. Wisdom will be required to make careful decisions that ignore political, sectional, and church-size interest groups, but which focus on what is best for the whole church. Such leaders need our support and prayers.

There is no stopping the change. Wise denominational leaders will lead the change, not respond to it after the fact. They will be proactive. They will not merely shut down one program or department after another without a strategic plan, but will get ahead of the curve and reinvent the denomination for the 21st century—before we get to that century. Most of all we hope they will have wisdom; wisdom to know *how* to reinvent the denomination for the 21st century.

"We're Not in Kansas Anymore..."

by Alan E. Nelson

L ike many of us raised in the church, there were times as a child when I was not so fond of our activism. One time I remember was on the Sunday nights "The Wizard of Oz" was aired. I couldn't watch more than the introduction because I had to go to church. Eventually I did get to see it and now my children have the video. Dorothy's classic line has been used *ad nauseum*, but was never more applicable than now in the church, "We're not in Kansas anymore." Whirlwind changes are spinning around us. There are evils in this new land. There are those masquerading as good wizards. But there are also wonderful, good, and beautiful things to see and do. While we try to understand the new dimension with the glasses of the old, we become frustrated. It is better if we start afresh; begin with the bare basics and think new thoughts.

Straining the metaphor a bit further, Dorothy eventually awakens, back in her home with Auntie Em and friends. She admits, "There's no place like home." Some Christians feel that the changes among our congregations are not home for them; they seem alien, strange, discomforting. But home for the Christian never has been a tradition, a style of music, or a format for ministry which fits our comfort zone. No, home for the believer is with the Holy Spirit, and God's Spirit is at the cutting-edge of making the gospel as contemporary and practical as ever. Unlike Dorothy, we will never be returning to Kansas. There's no hope of waking up, only to find that we've merely been dreaming. If we are to survive the non-Kansas environment, we are going to have to regain our familiarity with the movement of God.

For some of us, adjusting means knowing that we should stay just as we are and die with dignity. For others of us it means taking the risk of beginning a new church with tools and resources necessary to reduce the risk. For many of us, it means boldly casting the vision for *the new thing* amidst our old thing, to buck the status quo and branch out into new ventures within the existing ministry. God has never stopped doing new things. In that way, He is the same yesterday, today, and tomorrow.

Those of you who have read the words of this book and thought about the ideas of the writers, should recognize that The New Thing is not a stylistic approach to ministry which fits the Boomers or GenX. It goes beyond that. The New Thing is not a destination, some sort of modern ministry model. If that were the case, by the time this book was published and distributed, The New Thing would have been replaced by the next new thing or two. Rather, The New Thing is a mind-set, a way of understanding change and fluid motion in ministry. It has to do with reaching people in a post-modern society where the blur of change in values and technology affect us all. Now, perhaps as much or more than ever, people are interested in spiritual things. We have the opportunity to help them understand that God's Word and the way of Christ are the solutions to this quest.

The purpose of this book is to portray the template of 21st century ministry, as seen by progressive leaders in the holiness movement. A plethora of new ideas should be raised and addressed to help us see how things need to change in the future. Here are just a few out-of-the-box issues which progressive pastors and lay leaders are considering:

1. Why don't we see qualified lay people elected to places of district and general church positions, currently reserved only for ordained leaders?

2. Why don't we budget churches a flat 10% tithe that we expect from our parishioners, instead of convoluted and often significantly higher rates that will be difficult to justify to Boomers and Busters in leadership?

3. Why not design a style of missionary support where local churches align with people groups and specific missionaries, instead of general/generic missions?
4. Why not consider all church plants as missionary status for two to three years, granting benefits for those who invest in them?
5. Why not elect denominational people after potential voters have heard speeches, vision casting, or had the opportunity to discern the passion of the people for the potential ministry role and avoid politics, favoritism, or merely voting on looks?
6. What would a local church be like which hired a pastor specifically as a leader, and which hired staff for teaching, worship, and other forms of ministry vital for health? Who says the leader needs to be the preacher?
7. Why don't we move toward general church structures where a single leader casts vision as some denominations have, instead of a committee system where consensus tends to water down transformation and vision casting? Do we not trust our theology and system to raise up strong leaders and yet avoid a personality cult?

These are but examples of the type of questions which 21st century churches and members will need to be asking. They certainly possess the potential of rocking the boat, but so long as Jesus is in our boat, we need not fear capsizing. The avoidance of boat-rocking creates more of a likelihood of sinking during times like these.

"The church is moving rapidly toward a moment of decision, a defining moment. What are are the options? Simply, we can die because of our hidebound resistance to change or we can die in order to live. The reality is that the church is already on a direct course toward the first option. If the institutional church does nothing, which it is in fact good at doing, the choice has been made."[1] Regele talks about a subject which is akin to the Wesleyan heritage, dying to self-will, brokenness before God, total humility. A part of the dying process involves confession and repentance, which by its very etymology involves a change of mind. Regele continues, "The first act in our decision to die involves confession. We must acknowledge that we have sinned. We have loved death more than life. We have loved our traditions more than God. We have loved our institutions more than people."[2]

These are indeed harsh words, prophetic words, perhaps even stone-throwing, inciting words—but they need to be said. Our chances of avoiding local church death and movement death are dependent on our willingness to die to our traditions and infatuation with status quo and incremental change. To die in this sense does not mean disrespect for our forefathers and their ways. We must affirm our past and applaud those who did their share of risk taking and pioneering. But we cannot allow future generations to scorn us because we moved into a maintenance mode. If we do not intentionally, aggressively allow The New Thing to happen in our churches, our children, grandchildren, and great grandchildren will have the right to accuse us of robbing them of a meaningful, relevant theology which works just as well today as it did in Wesley's day and before. We must simply, yet with sacrifice, translate these beliefs into the walk and talk of our current culture.

The End/The Beginning

ENDNOTES

[1] Mike Regele, *Death of the Church,* p. 19.
[2] Ibid., pp. 212-213.

If you would like more information on the resources available at the Southwest Center for Leadership, or would like to order more copies of this book, contact us at:

Southwest Center for Leadership
10247 E. San Salvador
Scottsdale, AZ 85258
Tel. 602.614.0001
Fax. 602.614.0169
Email: lead@primenet.com

Bulk discounts on TNT books.